La Húkma Illa Lillah | Judgement Belongs To Allah Alone

Al-Khateeb | The Narrator

Not to be confused with the quraishian Suhayl ibn Amr, the one who drafted the Hudaybiyyah peace *deal*. As I am not human but rather a creature gifted with an interesting ability to *conceal*. A narrator who steps away from the viewpoints to which most individuals *kneel*. All so I can retell the story of Ìslàäm in a way that would suit the Abadiyah *ideal*.

As long ago there was a time where every mythological *plight*, was simply known as a shapeshifting spirit with unseen *might*. In this book we will enter an islamic realm that predates its default *school*. As I am a servant who shapes the twisted streams of imadjinnary *fuel*.

Imadjïnnation | Imagination

Tulpa, a mystical concept of Tibetan Buddhism in which an entity is formed through a strong spiritual *focus*. If your imadjïnnation is strong enough you might be able to create your own personal *hocus pocus*. The term can be translated to the word 'manifestation' often in the form of an imadjïnnary *friend*. In today's world however a tulpa is more likely to be classed as a figment of someone else's mentally unstable *pretend*.

Be wary of its symbol since it carries the power to change your perspective to no apparent *end*. In this book the symbol is used by an imadjïnnary narrator who wishes to help the reader *comprehend*.

Tulpa | Thoughtform

Djinn | The Concealed

Al-Sha'ir | The Poet

In Pre-Islamic Arabia it was often suggested or *believed*. That poetry was a tool used by us Djinns that can't be *perceived*. Using the likes of you as a mere vessel to tell stories that otherwise couldn't be *conceived*. As we are the true pillars that drive the ideas forever floating around inside your head so don't be *deceived*.

As there's always a risk to be influenced by a swarmy Djinn seeking to escape its hellfire *cage*. An evil that carries the burden of a shaitan's *rage*. Now as you finish reading these words and turn to the next *page*. You will read a series of verses from the divinely inspired quran translated by **I**, the imadjinnary *sage*.

The Servant Of Imadjinnation

The label 'Djinn' refers to 'the hidden' or an even better term would be 'the *concealed*'. The invisible shapeshifters with potential powers no human can naturally *wield*. Now step away from literalism as if you had Abadiyah in your *heart*. And imadjinn the shift as the people's endless failures to describe that which they were never able to see from the *start*.

The spirits of the *unseen* forever lurking behind every story in a manner almost *obscene*. The roots of all *mythology* that to this day still manage to influence your *psychology*. No matter what *ideology*, **we** have been the constant throughout the people's everchanging *chronology*.

Quran Verse 01 | The Opening

In name of Allah, most gracious & mer-
ciful of *all*

Praise be to Allah master of the universe
as I heed your *call*

For you truly are the most gracious &
merciful with no *downfall*

The lord of judgement day where the
people are sure to *bawl*

As we only praise you & seek thy aid
when backed against the *wall*

Guide us to the path where we safely
avoid the hellfire *fall*

The path straightforward where the
people stand equally *tall*

Not the path of wrath & disorientation
through whispers so *small*

Quran Surah 01 | Al-Fatiha

Bismillaah ar-Rahman ar-*Raheem*

Al hamdu lillaahi rabbil '*alameen*

Ar-Rahman ar-*Raheem*

Maaliki yaumid *Deen*

Iyyaaka na'abudu wa iyyaaka *nasta'een*

Ihdinas siraatal *mustaqeem*

Siraatal ladheena an 'amta' alaihim

Ghairil maghduubi' alaihim *waladaaleen*

Allah | God

Ìslàäm l The Religion Of P's (Pillars)

Quran Surah 109 | Al-Kafirun

Bismillaah ar-Rahman ar-*Raheem*

Qul ya ayyuha *alkafiroon*

La 'abudu ma *ta'abudoon*

Wala antum 'abidoona ma *a'abud*

Wala ana a'aabidun ma *a'aabadtum*

Wala antum a'abidoona ma *a'abud*

Lakum deenukum waliya deen

Quran Verse 109 | The Disbelievers

In name of Allah, most gracious & merciful of *all*

To those that reject the principle of faith I would like to *say*

That I will never adore that which you worship for I will not be lead *astray*
Nor do you have to adore that which I worship with all my *heart*

Once again I shall not worship that which you adore every *day*
Nor do you have to worship that which I adore from finish to *start*

For you have your beliefs as I have mine

Quran Verse 114 | The People

In name of Allah, most gracious & merciful of *all*

I vow to seek refuge with our lord more than my own *career*
The true master of the people forever present in our *atmosphere*

The one and only god whose reign will never *disappear*

Allah guard us from the evil suggestions of Iblis The *Insincere*
Whose devout subjects whisper dark thoughts into every *ear*
Of both Djinns and People with results often so *severe*

Quran Surah 114 | An-Naas

Bismillaah ar-Rahman ar-*Raheem*

Qul a'oodu birabbi *naas*

Maliki *naas*
Ilayhi *naas*

Min sharri alwaswasi alghan*naas*

Alladee yuwaswisu fee sudoori *naas*

Minal djinnati wa *naas*

Madhab | School Of Thought

Mecca | The Muhajir's Origin

Quran Surah 111 | Al-Masad

Bismillaah ar-Rahman ar-*Raheem*

Tabbat yada abee lahabin *watab*

Ma aghna Aanhu maluhu wama *kasab*

Sayasla naran thata *lahabin*

Waimraatuhu hammalata *alhatabi*

Fee jeediha hablun min *masadin*

Quran Verse 111 | The Palm Fiber

In name of Allaah, most gracious & merciful of *all*

Perish the two hands of Abu Lahab along with his damned *soul*

For none of his riches and glory will save him from hellfire's scorching *coal*

Forever shall he be left to burn in flames that engulf him as a *whole*

Flames forever fueled by his wife who carries the crackling *wood*

While a rope of palm fibre is worn as a noose around her neck for *good*

Al-Falaq | The Dawn

In name of Allah, most gracious & mer-
ciful of *all*

I vow to seek refuge with our lord who
masters the dawn that breaks our *day*.

To save us from the tricks of Iblisian
ideology hell-bent on leading us *astray*.

All so we may keep our peaceful balance
preserved from the darkness that *grows*

Larger and wider by the oracles that
practise the secret art of the *shadows*

The artform that feeds the envy of Iblis
The Insincere who we strongly *oppose*

Quran Surah 113 | Al-Falaq

Bismillaah ar-Rahman ar-*Raheem*

Qul a'oodu birabbil *falaq*

Min sharri ma *khalaq*

Wamin sharri ghasiqin ida *waqab*

Wamin sharri annaffathati fee *al'uqad*

Wamin sharri hasidin ida *hasad*

Yathrib | The Ansar's Haven

Quraish

The polytheistic tribe to which the islamic faith was bestowed upon *first*. Where dolls & statues were honored depending on the meccan's money hungry *thirst*.

A tribe of multiple **Banus** or **Houses** in the English *word*. In this chapter members of different spheres give their views that have yet to be *heard*.

Khadija

The first one to embrace the islamic message of unity through **ONE TRUE GOD**. A very rich woman who funded the first of all islamic campaigns as we praise her with *applaud*.

For she was without a doubt Muhammad's most favored *broad*. The time has come to learn about the birth and rise of ìs-láám through her *facade*.

01

Khadija Bint Khuwaylid I Umm-Muslimeen

They used to call me **Al-Ameerah, The Princess** of this quraishi alliance who carried Mecca's *pride*. Our tribal confederation consisted of 14 different **Banus, Houses** who all played a role in making sure the idolatrous rules were *applied*. My father Khuwaylid was a member of Banu Asad and also one of the richest merchants who firmly believed in Hubal's *guide*. But I myself was never interested in any idols for I always preferred an unseen *guide*.

When my father passed *away* he left his business to me so it would never *decay*. As he knew my brother Nawfal was a lion who would rid himself of any responsibility to get his *way*. I received criticism from every merchant as they found me unworthy of a profession in which I received equal *pay*. But their adversity only further empowered me to become the richest so I could have all the *say*. In the end my caravans *alone* equaled that of every other merchant combined as their jealousy was forever set in *stone*.

I was unsuccessfully married three times before I asked to wed Muhammad's *hand*. He agreed and our marriage was special for he was a man who carried a soul of the *grand*.

Umm-Muslimeen I Khadija Bint Khuwaylid

One Night At Mount Hira
610 J

Khadija Bint Khuwaylid I Umm-Muslimeen

There was one main thing that many meccans had forgotten about the Ka'aba forever shaped like a *square*. It was originally a house built by Abraham, a prophet who found guidance in Allah through the form of *prayer*. He built it along with his two *sons*, Ishmael the father of Arabs and Isaac who fathered the Jewish *ones*. But over time their influence was completely washed *away*. Leaving behind zero trace as the Ka'aba was now completely filled with 360 different deities whose statues would often *decay*.

360 statues who symbolised the 360 different tribes of Arabia at that particular *time*. Each tribe traveled to Mecca as a pilgrim to worship their chosen idol who they saw as *sublime*. Mecca had truly become the central hub of both idolatrous worship and caravan *trade*. Until Muhammad was inspired by **Jibreel, Gabriel** who possessed not a single form of *shade*. Muhammad would endlessly shiver inside mount Hira's *cave*. While he kept receiving divine inspiration that was strong enough to liberate any *slave*.

I was the first to accept Muhammad's message of *peace*, and my friend Lubaba joined soon after his poetic *release*.

Umm-Muslimeen I Khadija Bint Khuwaylid

02

Khadija The Great
556 - 620 J

Khadija Bint Khuwaylid I Umm-Muslimeen

When my brother Nawfal tied up Talhah and Abu-Bakr for everyone to *see*. It annoyed me so much that I ended up slapping him accross the face until I was filled with *glee*. When he wished to respond I threatened to hire an assassin who would slice him to a merciless *degree*. He ended up bowing his head and ran back to his home as if he were a puny little *flea*. In truth I was pretty happy to witness that Nawfal believed my *plea*. For if he proved to be too much of a nuisance, an execution would take place *by my decree*.

Every *day* I *pray* and hope that the almighty Allah would free us from their idolatrous *error*. For the weakest of us could no longer bear their vile persecutions of *terror*. That was the main reason why I inspired Uthman to convince Muhammad on a path to The Abyssinian's *land*. Where a compassionate Negus ruled the kingdom with his Christian *hand*. A peaceful place where the weakest of us could seek refuge away from the hatred of our *homeland*.

I must say I truly was impressed to hear that Jafar was able to undo that nobleman's hideous *lie*. As his recitation of the quranic verses made the Negus and his bishops *cry*.

Umm-Muslimeen I Khadija Bint Khuwaylid

Khadija Bint Khuwaylid I Umm-Muslimeen

Of the fourteen different houses that made up Mecca's tribal *scene*. Four of them developed from a common ancestor whose four sons each developed a house of which the DJïnns were very *keen*. Banu Abd-Shams that was now under the stern leader Utbah's *command*. Banu Nawfal with no relation at all to my brother, the lion who marched with pride through the quraishi *sand*. Banu Mutallib who raised his little nephew Shaibah after his older brother Hashim passed away completely *unplanned*.

And lastly Banu Hashim to which I chose to belong after I demanded to wed Muhammad's *hand*. During the boycott the Hashims and Mutallibs were banished all *together*. I had to give up all my wealth to make sure we didn't starve to death as we constantly felt under the *weather*. And when Abu-Taleb died I knew we were no longer *protected*.

So I asked Muhammad to preach beyond our home since the meccans felt *unaffected*. It backfired and he was bullied away with violence and *hate*. But thankfully Mu'tim of Banu Nawfal escorted him back through Mecca's *gate*. I embraced him one last time before I met my untimely *fate*.

Umm-Muslimeen I Khadija Bint Khuwaylid

04

05

Khadija Bint Khuwaylid I Umm-Muslimeen

The emigration of meccans to yathribi *land*, after the warring Arab factions of that city chose to bury their head in the *sand*. They did so by embracing Muhammad's message without *pretend*. Which took away the opportunity to kill a fellow brother as a means to justify their personal *end*. The **Bayah** at Mount Aqabah where 75 pilgrims from all yathribi *tribes*. Became Muslims to ensure a definitve halt to their tireless warfare often silenced by *bribes*.

Upon hearing of this secret **Pledge** the quraishi leaders went mad with *fear*. Giving the go ahead to kill Muhammad before he could reach Yathrib's *atmosphere*. But the messenger was warned and Ali chose to protect his *rear*.

When his nephew had finished his quest in Mecca he set forth to Yathrib where Muhammad eagerly awaited *him*. After he fearlessly sacrificed his life to save the messenger from a fate so *grim*. They became brothers in faith much to my daughter Fatima's *satisfaction*. And one year later Muhammad received divine inspiration telling him the two young ones should wed for their *faction*. Upon doing so many saw Ali as the one to succeed him in *action*.

Umm-Muslimeen I Khadija Bint Khuwaylid

Khadija Bint Khuwaylid I Umm-Muslimeen

In the beginning Muhammad made his men settle at the first well they could *see*. But one of them suggested they march further to the wells near the rival as that was *key*. To block them from water and fuel our victorious *glee*.

Before the battle smaller skirmishes between the two had already been *fought*. After the Quraish had seized personal Muslim assets that could never again be *bought*. So the Muslims retaliated by launching a series of caravan raids to settle the *score*. So the quraishi leaders would feel uneasy making their paranoia continually *soar*. After a while actual blood was *spilled*, resulting in a declaration of battle where many soldiers would find themselves *killed*.

The victory at the wells of Badr that placed the Muslims on Arabia's *radar*. A battle that the Quraish had originally envisioned as an easy win but they underestimated Ali who fought like a shooting *star*. The Muslim army made up about a third of the quraishi *one*. But Allah's fate strengthened their conviction for they all felt invincible as the battle was easily *won*. After killing so many quraishi noblemen Mecca's power structure had come *undone*.

Umm-Muslimeen I Khadija Bint Khuwaylid

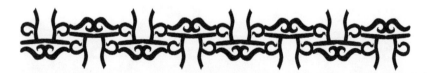

06

07

Khadija Bint Khuwaylid I Umm-Muslimeen

Our side was still in a state of euphoria after our previous victory at Badr which put us on Arabia's *radar*. So much so that they were already bragging about a second win before they even started to *spar*. The realists among the Muslims already knew they would fall to **Al-Walid, The Loner** who mastered his use of the lance as a true *star*. For he showed more fear towards Allah than the Muslims who *pray* more than once a *day*. A devastating loss that almost saw Muhammad die in the most barbaric *way*.

The ceremony began with another melee but this time Hind was there to empower the quraishi *side*. Her soothsaying ability leaving a lasting effect in a battle that was no where near *tied*. For in the end the Muslims lost all grounds when they abandoned Muhammad to save their own *hide*. But at least this battle gave birth to our first female warrior who marched forth with defensive *stride*.

Taking several arrows and striking blows to protect Muhammad who she saw as the almighty Allah's final *guide*. In the end he forgave the Muslims after he was ordered *to*. For a victory only happens when Allah wills it to be *true*.

Umm-Muslimeen I Khadija Bint Khuwaylid

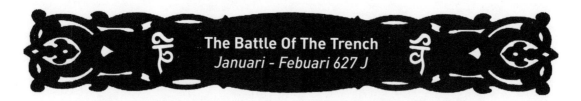

The Battle Of The Trench
Januari - Febuari 627 J

Khadija Bint Khuwaylid I Umm-Muslimeen

Before Muhammad emigrated to Yathrib and took charge
of *action*. It was a city that consisted of multiple Jewish
Banus and two Arab ones who hated each other's faction.
Banu Khazraj and Aws, who originally emigrated from
Yemen and battled each other as a violent *reaction*. To the
endless series of unjust crimes that were often settled by
a blood money *transaction*. Muhammad had set up a char-
ter that everyone was asked to *sign*, in an honest attempt
to make everyone's personal interests perfectly *align*.

But Ibn-Salul did everything he *could*, to banish the mes-
senger back to his meccan *hood*. His instigations went so
far that two Jewish tribes found themselves *expelled*. Banu
Nadir and Banu Qaynuqa who decided that the terms of
the charter should no longer be *upheld*. After their expul-
sion they moved to Khaybar and traveled all across Arabia
to gather a large idolatrous *army*. Then they marched for
battle alongside the son of war who had a face so *swarmy*.

Thankfully Salman had already been freed from his *chain*.
Giving him the chance to prove his worth as he used the
mighty power of creativity that belonged to his *brain*.

Umm-Muslimeen I Khadija Bint Khuwaylid

08

The Imadjïnnary Narrator
J 627 - 05 H

Khadija Bint Khuwaylid I Umm-Muslimeen

A peace treaty set up after the Muslims were denied entrance to Mecca for the pilgrimage *season*. Causing a political tension that Suhayl Ibn Amr managed to settle by using a necessary amount of *reason*. A treaty with an expiration date of ten years. Securing the safety of both sides as there were no more retaliation *fears*. Every citizen was able to join their preferred *side*. Without fear of punishment for that would surely cause yet another great *divide*.

During the treaty the Muslims finally had a necessary chance to *rest*. Giving the **Ümmah, Community** a way to prove they were able to pass Allah's *test*. Muhammad set out scouts to find new recruits all accross the arabian *sand*. They would often ride for days on end through the amazing golden brown *land*. Over time the number of converts continually *grew*. Until one day the autonomous Banu Khuza'a chose to join our side of the *queue*. Giving their rivals a chance to join the idolatrous quraishi *crew*.

After one thing led to another innocent blood was *spilled*. Giving Muhammad a true reason to march for Mecca's *guild*. A conquest that saw the Muslim dream *fulfilled*.

Umm-Muslimeen I Khadija Bint Khuwaylid

Khadija Bint Khuwaylid I Umm-Muslimeen

The treaty was violated by Banu Bakr the allies of the quraishi *side*. After they were informed that their rivals Banu Khuza'a had joined the Muslim *pride*. A massacre at a place called Al-Wateer where no man was allowed to *hide*. Upon hearing of the attack Muhammad's stomache had turned upside *down*. And the son of war's plea to accept a vast sum of blood money only made the messenger's eyebrows *frown*. He chose to respond with a very simple no that ended Abu-Sufyan's useless *negotiation*.

He brought together his entire army and marched forth towards Mecca's *station*. The city of polytheism would soon again transform into a place of monotheist *prostration*. Ali was given the black flag to enter the gates of Mecca *first*, clearing the way for the Abyssinian's confrontational *thirst*. After every noblemen publicly converted for everyone to *see*. He climbed on top of the Ka'aba and called everyone to prayer as Allah's words filled his soul with *glee*.

Never again will the city of Ka'aba refrain from a monotheist *decree*. Praise be upon Allah who sent Muhammad as a mercy to the world even the DJ'inns would *agree*.

Umm-Muslimeen I Khadija Bint Khuwaylid

10

Bãnu House Of

The very prophet himself in which he was born and *raised*. From the point of view of both his nephew and uncle will their house feel *praised*.

As it always was a safe space for He Who Himself Was Never *Phased*. By the reality of his life as a human displaced from cradle to *grave*. All praise Muhammad The *Brave*.

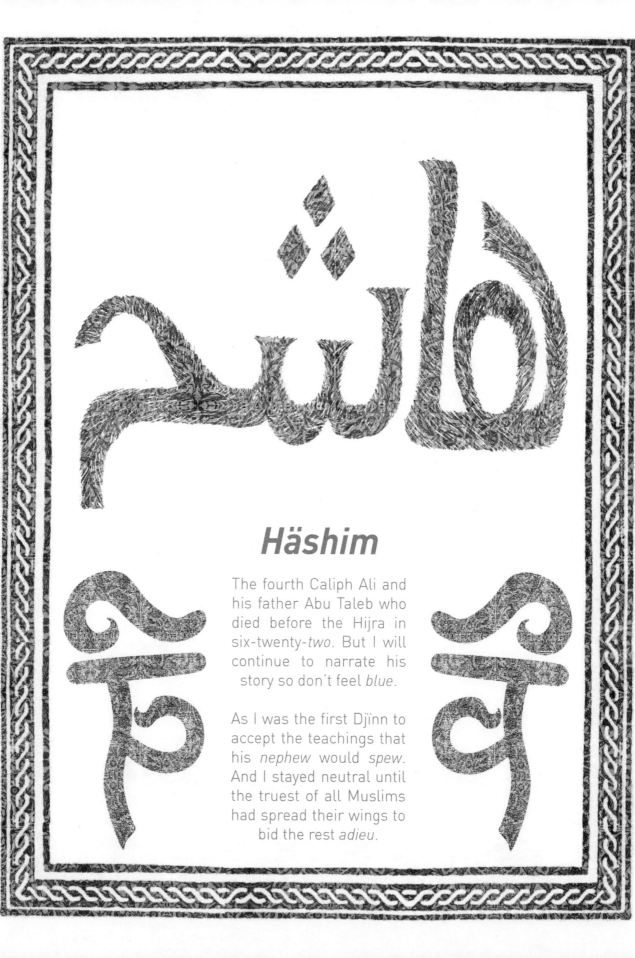

Häshim

The fourth Caliph Ali and his father Abu Taleb who died before the Hijra in six-twenty-*two*. But I will continue to narrate his story so don't feel *blue*.

As I was the first Djinn to accept the teachings that his *nephew* would *spew*. And I stayed neutral until the truest of all Muslims had spread their wings to bid the rest *adieu*.

Ali Ibn Abi-Taleb I Taliba

The messenger's most favored nephew who was often deemed special by the Quraish because of my singular *birth*. Inside the Ka'aba with an audience of 360 supernatural deities that visibly roam the *earth*. Fatima, the lion's daughter entered the shrine and came out three days later after silently conceiving me as if she were a *mime*. When Muhammad held me in his arms my eyes opened up for the very first *time*. He asked my mother if she had already thought of a name for her new child so *sublime*.

She answered that the deities who helped her with my effortless birth suggested that **Ali** would be a good name for *me*. It means **The Exalted One** which was quite a suitable title even the messenger would *agree*.

I lived in my parental household until I was about six years of *age*. Then famine came along and my father could no longer support us all much to his *outrage*. So I was taken in by Muhammad and my older brother Jafar lived with my uncle Al-Abbas who earned a healthy *wage*. Muhammad was the one who raised me into the man I am *today*. So I'll make sure to uphold his legacy by never being led *astray*.

Taliba I Ali Ibn Abi-Taleb

Abu-Taleb Ibn Abdul-Muttalib I Al-Hashimi

I was the official head of Banu Hashim where my father Shaibah was placed in his uncle Mutallib's care from a very young *age*. After his father Hashim had died rather suddenly while returning from a business trip in which he was earning his *wage*. People often used to think Shaibah was his uncle's servant so they nicknamed him Abdul-Muttalib even though he was never locked inside a *cage*.

Muhammad's father Abd Allah and his great-grandfather Hashim died in the same sudden *way*. So when he was placed in my care I felt as though history was repeating itself in both pleasure and *dismay*. In my entire life I had never seen a boy like Muhammad *before*. Displaced from the day he was born but never did he blame anyone for being dealt such a lousy *score*. No matter what he would always believe in a straightforward way of thinking instead of the idolatrous ideas that Arabia used to *adore*.

I saw him as my very own *son*, especially when he made sure my children would never starve as another *one*. Even though I had a hard time to believe the things he *said*. I still chose to protect him when people aimed for his *head*.

Al-Hashimi I Abu-Taleb Ibn Abdul-Muttalib

12

Ali Ibn Abi-Taleb I Taliba

I was the second person to accept his message and the first convert amongst the male *kind*. Muhammad, Khadija and I would often wake up at dawn and pray in front of the Ka'aba with our souls completely *aligned*. This religion started within our **Bayt**, **The House** that would eventually spread its teachings to all of *mankind*. Then came the conversion of his dear friend Abu-Bakr the truthful man with a righteously intelligent *mind*.

As the list of converts started to *grow*, the Quraish decided to persecute us in a grand *show*. I remember very well when Nawfal the lion had tied together Abu-Bakr and his wealthy friend Talha in front of everyone they *know*. The members of their house simply laughed and abandoned them as if they were a *foe*. The very moment I found out about this I swore an oath to Allah that I would be the one to make Nawfal reap that which he hath chosen to *sew*.

The persecutions became too much for the weaker ones including my older *brother*. Who successfully led the second wave of emigrants to Abyssinia where the Negus wept after hearing his quranic recitation of Mary the *mother*.

Taliba I Ali Ibn Abi-Taleb

Abu-Taleb Ibn Abdul-Muttalib I Al-Hashimi

Muhammad's message truly brought the Quraish a great deal of *fear*. It even went so far that the meccan leaders offered him the throne if he made his poetic words *disappear*. But he swiftly refused for he believed Allah to be forever present in our *atmosphere*. When he said no the Quraish drafted up a scroll to exile us all away from *here*. Every last member of Banu Hashim and Mutallib was placed under this meccan *boycott* whether they had chosen to adopt Muhammad's religion or *not*.

Only Abu-Lahab was free of exile since he left our house after the Quraish realised his alliance could be *bought*. For two years we lived as people of the *poor*, until Mu'tim of Banu Nawfal ended the treaty by settling the *score*. Although he didn't believe in Muhammad's *vision*, he was convinced that no one should suffer an attack of *precision*.

Not so long after the boycott ended I found myself falling rather *ill*. In my final moments of life I tried one last time to get both sides of the meccan coin to *chill*. But I was unsuccessful in doing so as it simply wasn't planned in Allah's *will*. I pray that Muhammad survives the quraishi *kill*.

Al-Hashimi I Abu-Taleb Ibn Abdul-Muttalib

14

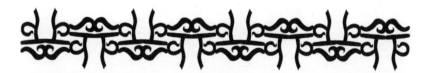

Ali Ibn Abi-Taleb I Taliba

Muhammad had entered my chambers at night after he had a horrifying vision that left him covered with *sweat*. He had received divine inspiration from Allah who warned the messenger of an upcoming *threat*. The strongest fighters of the Quraish would enter our home and murder him without *wait*. And so I more than gladly offered to risk my own life to save him from such a terrible *fate*.

While he and Abu-Bakr escaped to Yathrib I covered myself under the blankets of his *bed*. When the fighters lifted up the fabric it was revealed to be me *instead*. This *led* to an angry form of confusion that caused Abu-Jahl's eyes to turn completely *red*. Killing me was a step too far for the Quraish as they still loved my late father Abu-Taleb may Allah have mercy for the *dead*.

After that night I stayed in Mecca to tie up all of his loose *strings*. By rightfully giving back the properties assigned to him as a merchant among other *things*. Then I left for my Hijra along with both of my Fatimas and two other women who were fed up with quraishi *kings*. In Yathrib I was named brother to Muhammad, the prophet with *wings*.

Taliba I Ali Ibn Abi-Taleb

Asadullah I Lion Of Allah
594 - 661 J

16

Ali Ibn Abi-Taleb I Taliba

The battle commenced with a three man melee from each *side*. Ali, Hamza and Ubaidah of the Hashims represented the Muslim's *pride*. While Utbah, Shaybay and Walid of the Abd-Shams were chosen as champions to defend the quraishi *divide*. Ubaidah was injured but he still brought Shaybah to a *defeat*. While Ali quickly slaughtered Walid in quite an impressive *feat*. And lastly Utbah was completely destroyed by Hamza who could kill anyone in a *heartbeat*.

After the three were slaughtered arrows from both sides started flying with *speed*. While Taliba marched for Naw-fal to honor his pledge towards Allah's *creed*. When the two locked *eyes* they lifted their swords to the *skies*. Then they marched towards each other to battle it out like real *men*. In the end Ali managed to slay the lion of the Quraish there and *then*. Once Nawfal dropped dead to the ground Taliba had decided to march forth in battle all over *again*.

He managed to impress everyone with the results of his first *battle*. Slaughtering about 27 soldiers as if they were all part of the *cattle*. If he would be able to keep up with the *kill*, he might even be granted the sword of Allah's *will*.

Taliba I Ali Ibn Abi-Taleb

Ali Ibn Abi-Taleb I Taliba

How on earth could those stupid soldiers disobey Muhammad's *cries*. I always knew greed was able to consume even the most pious of *guys*. But I never expected it to happen to our faithful *allies*. Thankfully we were able to save my brother Muhammad from a fate of certain *demise*. As his loyal knight and I were aided by Nusaybah, a female convert originally from the Jewish *skies*. But let us never forget Mus'ab the grateful one pretending to be Muhammad while wearing a cloak of *disguise*.

As he distracted the quraishi fighters by loudly yelling **Allahu Akbar, Allah Is Great** with all his *heart*. He was killed by a spear thrown by a man whose aim was often deemed a work of *art*. As the battle ended Muhammad stood over his body now without *life*. "To Allah We Belong And To Allah We Return All Along" wailed his grieving *wife*.

He gave his final words and repayed me for breaking my sable in half during the *fight*. By giving me the sword he received from Gabriel an angel of purified *light*. As of now there is no brave youth except *Ali*, and Zulfiqhar is the only blade which renders the true service to slice *thee*.

Taliba I Ali Ibn Abi-Taleb

Asadullah I Lion Of Allah
594 - 661 J

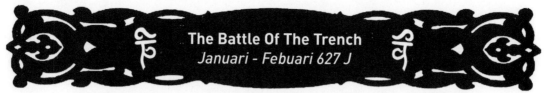

18

Ali Ibn Abi-Taleb / Taliba

Zulfiqhar, the angel *blade* that was given to Muhammad when Hamza demanded to see Gabriel, the angel without *shade*. He was able to see a shiny foot for a mere moment or *two*, until he completely passed out as his mind went *adieu*. A blade that only strengthened Ali's power and *speed*. The rumors of this sword had even spread throughout Mecca as the idolatrous citizens were highly *intrigued*.

The sword itself was shaped as an ancient scimitar with a double-edged *point*. Able to slice someone in half without ever managing to *disappoint*. A sword unlike any you've ever *seen*, made of an exalted steel of which Ali was very *keen*. No one stood a chance to beat him in a *fight*, for any opponent would find their lives at the mercy of his *might*. As it was a weapon graced with Allah's eternal *light*. And no one could beat him for he followed an invincible *plight*.

When the Persian suggested to dig the trenches the Muslims found themselves with a hopeful *thrill*. As the Quraish immediately lost all their leverage forcing them to send a champion that Ali could *kill*. The quraishi Amr Ibn Abd Al-Wud was the true champion who fell by his merciless *skill*.

Taliba / Ali Ibn Abi-Taleb

Ali Ibn Abi-Taleb I Taliba

All we wanted to do was go to Mecca to perform our pilgrimage as a basic Arab *right*. But we were blocked at every turn by the Quraish who opposed it with all their *might*. A solution had to be found immediately or the tensions would escalate into another *fight*. We were stationed in Hudaybiyyah, a town nearby the meccan *city*. Then we sent Uthman the generous one to reason with the quraishi *committee*. But they ended capturing him *instead*.

Muhammad then brought all of us together under a tree and *said*: "I want each of you to step before me and vow that if not returned safely to us we will avenge Uthman's *head!*" The Quraish quickly succeeded and brought him out alongside Suhayl the narrator of Mecca's *tribes*. It was often said that he was the only meccan who did not accept the customised standard of political *bribes*.

Muhammad had me write down our terms of the Hudaybiyyah treaty as I was also one of his regular *scribes*. But I did not agree at all with Suhayl's request to erase my brother's true prophetic *title*. Even if it meant we would lose the chance for a peace treaty that was truly *vital*.

Taliba I Ali Ibn Abi-Taleb

Ali Ibn Abi-Taleb l Taliba

After the Hudaybiyyah treaty was *signed*, Muhammad and Ali's souls became perfectly *aligned*. Throughout the *years* the messenger gave him countless assignments to rid him of all *fears*. For only Allah would be deserving of such a powerful *emotion*, as Ali was the exalted youth who carried the bravest of all *devotion*. Whenever he was given a clear *order* he executed it without causing public *disorder*.

The battle of Khaybar was the one in which he proved himself beyond *imadjïnnation*. As he was assigned to conquer the Jewish oasis that gave asylum to Banu Nadir the ones who possessed a truly vengeful *frustration*. At first Ali had decided to do so without battle so he used the almighty Allah's *dictation*. But the leaders of Khaybar still chose to plunge into battle to preserve their strictly Jewish *nation*.

Two champions were sent to face the brave youth who carried the angel *blade*. At first the leading commander Harith stepped forward while remaining completely *unafraid*. After he was sliced rather quickly Marhab rose up to avenge his brother's bloody *shade*. After the battles Taliba was renamed **Asadullah, The Lion Of Allah**'s *crusade*.

Taliba l Ali Ibn Abi-Taleb

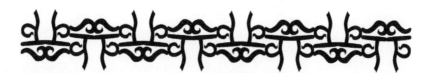

Bãnu House Of

Abu-Bakr, the very first Caliph to rule after Muhammad's untimely *end*. He was named 'As-Siddiq' for The Truthful speeches he delivered to the Ümmah without *pretend*.

But no need to rush so for now he's tied *together*. To Talhah, the dark skinned merchant who would toy with his ring when feeling under the *weather*.

Tãym

Al-Qareenayn or 'The Two Tied Together' was given to them as a *label*. After being humiliated by Nawfal, the lion whose hatred for them remained *stable*.

From the first preachings to his final *breath*. By the sword of Ali & the angel of *death*. Look no further than this *part*, to realise Abu-Bakr was an honest muslim at the *start*.

Abu-Bakr As-Siddiq I Siddiqi

A light skinned man from a family tree highly invested in the cloth *trade*. When I was a young boy my parents sent me to the bedouin deserts where I developed a fondness for the camels that sat in the *shade*. As I would play around with their calves while forever remaining *unafraid*. When I was ten years old my father took me to Syria in one of his caravan *expeditions*. Muhammad, aged twelve at the time was also there but we didn't speak as back then we still had different *ambitions*. But we treated each other with respect in accordance with our hospitable *traditions*.

Like the other rich kids of meccan *society*. I was taught to master the skills of literacy as they were a sign of *notoriety*. I had a distinct fondness for poetry in every *variety*. As it was the only good thing about this idolatrous *anxiety*.

When I grew older I decided to become a cloth merchant to uphold the family business I *admired*. And over time I had become so good at it that it turned into everything that my heart *desired*. But then I saw how Muhammad's message had helped Ali become so *inspired*. Immediately after seeing that I felt as though my conversion was *required*.

Siddiqi I Abu-Bakr As-Siddiq

As-Siddiq I The Truthful
573 - 634 J

One Night At Mount Hira
610 J

22

Talhah Ibn-Ubaidullah I Al-Taymi

Dark skinned, with a narrow nose on a handsome face and even wavier *hair*. A merchant who wished to travel the entire world to build his wealth with *flair*. I wanted to leave behind an estate of no less than 30 million dirhams for I had more than one *heir*. But even with such a luxury life I felt a hollow void deep within my *soul*. A void that started to fill itself up as I felt inspired by Muhammad's *goal*. For he preached the lessons I encountered while working *abroad*. Upon hearing his recitation I began to see him as the messenger of Allah who was anything but a *fraud*.

Siddiqi my fellow of the Taym clan had converted right after Ali, the exalted *one*, his children quickly followed except for his eldest *son*. Soon after I demanded him to bring me before Muhammad the *wise*. So I could pledge my loyalty to him by stating the **Shahada** before his *eyes*:

Ash-hadu an laa ilaaha illallahu
Wa ash-hadu anna Muhammadan rasulullah

I bear witness that Allah is the one and only *god*
And that Muhammad is the final prophet I *applaud*

Al-Taymi I Talhah Ibn-Ubaidullah

Talhah The Merchant
594 - 656 J

Abu-Bakr As-Siddiq I Siddiqi

I remember the time that Nawfal tied us together as if it were *yesterday*. Everyone mocked us and not a single person tried to defend us from the public's *dismay*. We were deemed unworthy of protection until Ali rescued us after his grand *entree*. Using his notorious uncle Hamza to intimade Nawfal in the most effective *way*. As a man of a higher class I never really knew what it was like to have my hands tied at someone else's *display*. No wonder the slaves were adhering to Muhammad's message without a single *delay*. I heard of their persecutions suffered at the hands of their masters who sought to lead them *astray*.

And so I decided to buy as many slaves as I could by using my *wealth*. To then free them so that one day they may regain their *health*. I bought about eight slaves including Bilal the bushy haired man with impeccable *stealth*.

As he never took the words of Allah in *vain* during Umaya The Obese's torture sessions of the *insane*. If it were up to me, all men and women would be freed from their *chain*. As I now found the entire process to be *inhumane*. Hopefully I will succeed in doing so with little to no *pain*.

Siddiqi I Abu-Bakr As-Siddiq

Talhah Ibn-Ubaidullah I Al-Taymi

With the death of both Khadija and Abu-Taleb the messenger found himself lost in *translation*. The uncontrollable crying even started to disrupt his divine *narration*. Everyday I would pray twice as much to ask Allah to bring Muhammad's body, mind and soul back to *salvation*. For he had already gone through so much during the Hashimi boycott which left him *poor*. But nevertheless he still managed to preach his islamic message as Allah hath deemed it to be his prophetic *chore*. I had to find a way to relieve him of the destructive sorrow that shook up his very *core*.

I tried everything I could to inspire him to get back up on his two *feet*. But nothing worked until his uncle's wife Lubaba bore a son with a face so *sweet*. Muhammad's eyes lit up as he had found another angel that he could *treat*. The very moment he held him in his arms he rose up as if the entire mourning process was a mere *deceit*.

"When the older generation dies *away*. This young one shall inspire the followers with a vast sea of knowledge so their faith may never *decay*." Those were the words he *said*, to describe Ibn-Abbas as he kissed him on his *head*.

Al-Taymi I Talhah Ibn-Ubaidullah

Abu-Bakr As-Siddiq I Siddiqi

Muhammad came to me in the middle of the night and told me about his *dream*. So we packed up our belongings and escaped to unravel their murderous *scheme*. We entered a cave five miles from Mecca to hide from the mercenary *stream*. As the Quraish had promised great reward for the one that killed us without *wait*.

Three days I spent worrying that the two of us would meet our untimely *fate*. But Muhammad assured me of our safety as he knew that we were shielded by the presence of Allah the *great*. When the tensions died down we set forth our journey to forever escape the meccan's *hate*.

When we finally arrived in Yathrib we were welcomed with open *arms*. The people even renamed the city to **Al-Madinat Ul-Nabi, The City Of The Prophet** in response to Muhammad's *charms*. Over time it was shortened to **Al-Madina, The City** where Muhammad had taken charge of *action*. He made a man named Khaarijah my brother in faith to prevent any future *distraction*. This happened with every single one of the **Sahabas, Companions** originating from each gender and *faction*.

Siddiqi I Abu-Bakr As-Siddiq

25

Talhah Ibn-Ubaidullah I Al-Taymi

I remember the time I met Muhammad and Siddiqi on their way to Yathrib as if it were *yesterday*. They were hiding inside a cave for three days to escape the mercenary swords of *decay*. I gave them some syrian garments I had lying in my caravan so they could modestly continue on their *way*. While I myself marched for Mecca where the majority of its citizens still found themselves led *astray*.

There I completed my affairs and emigrated both my and Siddiqi's family to Yathrib so we could all live in *peace*. But sadly the Quraish had unjustly seized Muslim assets to make sure the tribalist tensions would never *cease*. So Muhammad started sending scouts to raid the meccan caravans until actual blood was *spilled*. Then I was assigned to locate Abu-Sufyan's caravan along with my brother in faith Sa'id a man who was highly *skilled*.

Because of this difficult task the two of us were unable to fight in the badrian battle that was won by our *side*. But upon arriving in Medina we were still given an equal share of the *divide*. For our role was crucial in securing a victory that gave the Quraish a necessary kick up their *backside*.

Al-Taymi I Talhah Ibn-Ubaidullah

Abu-Bakr As-Siddiq I Siddiqi

We had lost a battle to which Allah had granted us a victorious *right*. But sadly both fear and greed had given way for us to ignore Muhammad's *plight*. I among many had abandoned my post while Ali, Talhah and Nusaybah protected the messenger alongside his loyal *knight*. But I returned immediately after my daughters encouraged me to pick up my weapon and *fight*. I had to hear their empowering words for as a merchant I was never graced with a soldier's *light*. Talhah on the other hand had picked up certain skills while travelling through the eastern *night*.

Al-Walid, The Loner with impeccable tactical skills that brought us to a decisive *defeat*. I shall pray with all my heart so that one day you may find yourself joining our side of the *street*. As Allah hath deemed you to be a skillful warrior of the highest *elite*.

We buried our fallen on the battlefield after the Quraish had *won*. About 65 of our brethren had died including Mus'ab the grateful *one*. "Among the believers are *those* who truly upheld their pledge to Allah who truly *knows*" was what Muhammad had said to his wailing wife and *son*.

Siddiqi I Abu-Bakr As-Siddiq

As-Siddiq I The Truthful
573 - 634 J

The Battle Of The Trench
Januari - Febuari 627 J

Talhah Ibn-Ubaidullah I Al-Taymi

Because I had missed the first battle my eagerness for the second one was very *strong*. And when our soldiers fled their post I stayed close to the messenger to save him from any *wrong*. Together with the other warriors I protected Muhammad with all my *heart*. And when an arrow was about to hit him in the face I intercepted it with my hand as if it were a moment of *art*. A move that left two of my fingers paralyzed as if they were numb from the *start*.

In total I took about 75 hits to prevent any *harm*, for I truly believed Muhammad to be Allah's final merciful *charm*. As soon as all of my wounds had *healed*, the Khuza'a riders decided to set foot on our *field*. Warning us of the quraishi legion who sought to break our defensive *shield*. But in the end it was they who had eventually chosen to *yield*.

I thank the first Persian convert for his idea that brought us the *win*. It seemed as though it was only yesterday that he was still chained by that medinan Jew with a *grin*. As soon as he met Muhammad he bowed down and pledged his loyalty as if he had seen a heavenly *DJïnn*. Muhammad then helped him up and vowed to free him of any past *sin*.

Al-Taymi I Talhah Ibn-Ubaidullah

28

Talhah The Merchant
594 - 656 J

Abu-Bakr As-Siddiq I Siddiqi

In Hudaybiyyah I was worried sick about the survival of Uthman for he was sent as an envoy by my *suggestion*. When the quraishi delegates refused to answer us we all gathered and pledged our lives without *question*. **Bayat Ash-Shajarah, The Pledge Of The Tree** that brought the Quraish incredible *fear*. They quickly returned him to us and had Suhayl work with Muhammad to draft up a treaty necessary for a peaceful *atmosphere*.

When he requested that Muhammad should erase his title Ali refused for reasons that were *unclear*. However the messenger erased it himself as the Quraish had never acknowledged his prophetic *career*. And he knew that peace would make countless new recruits *appear*. Among them my eldest son chose our side with a mindset so *clear*.

We sat together and talked all night about our decisions of the *past*. Apparently at the badrian battle he had the chance to slay me but he abandoned that *forecast*. I as a truthful individual told him that if the tables were turned I would've martyred him with one *blast*. But he already knew that as my tactical decisions were always *steadfast*.

Siddiqi I Abu-Bakr As-Siddiq

29

Talhah Ibn Ubaydullah I Al-Taymi

At first it seemed as though the treaty would remain intact for the entire ten *years*. But that changed rather quickly after the massacre that left many of us in dire *tears*. The autonomous Khuza'a faction had chosen to join our side of the *street*. And the Bakr faction preferred to ally with the Quraish as the two were rivals forever seeking to *compete*. From the very beginning both sides had chosen to hate each other as a personal *treat*. Another blood feud that managed to make Arabia's essence feel highly *incomplete*.

One day the Bakr warriors were in the mood to disregard the peace treaty's terms so they could shed their enemy's *blood*. And so they camped in a place named Al-Wateer and waited for the Khuza'a men to travel accros the earthly *mud*. All so they could swiftly attack them so that a barbaric river of bloody red was able to *flood*.

Abu-Sufyan tried to do whatever he could so that Muhammad would forgive such a hateful *deed*. But it failed since the messenger was never blinded by the concept of merciless *greed*. So every offer to pay for the damage that was done was refused by him as a way of honoring his *creed*.

Al-Taymi I Talhah Ibn Ubaydullah

30

Bãnu House Of

Umar, the second Caliph
handpicked by 'As-Siddiq'
since he wrote it into his
will. A raw individual that
never let his feelings *spill*.
In public that is for deep
inside his martyred *soul*.

He teared up everytime
he failed his final *goal*. To
end the hungers and in-
justices of this evil world
as a *whole*. In his eyes all
had to play their *role*.

Ádiy

Al-Shefaa, whose given name was Layla, a woman so *wise*. Learning the skill of writing when it was barely mastered by twenty meccan *guys*.

Bazaar-Inspector in Medina during Umar's *reign*. Her wisdom even made her win the prophet's respect what a *brain*. He'd often ask her for feedback and she'd never *abstain*.

Umar Ibn Al-Khattab I Khattabo

I was born into a middle class family of Banu Adiy which was responsible for tribal council and *arbitration*. When I was younger I used to tend to my father's camels without a single form of *compensation*. He was a cruel man who overworked me into exhaustion and when I refused he would beat me mercilessly much to my *frustration*.

Eventually I started to learn how to fend for *myself*, and fearing for his life was what he did to *himself*. I had become a stone cold *killer*. And to me the idolatrous dolls were only there to suggest a meccan *pillar*. As The Abrahamians were the ones that built the Ka'aba forever shaped like a *square*. Dare to deny them and I'll demand permission to strike off your head so *beware*. For consuming the strongest liquors was what I personally considered as *prayer*. **Al-Walid, The Loner** and I were cousins and we always used to come together to drink and *swear*.

After my cowardly father died I had become head of the arbitrary faction without *scare*. But back then, right and wrong had no import for *me*. As I was often considered a son of **Abu-Jahl, The Father Of Ignorance** for all to *see*.

Khattabo I Umar Ibn Al-Khattab

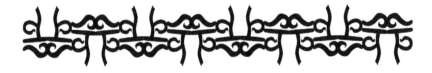

One Night At Mount Hira
610 J

Al-Shefaa Bint Abdullah I Umm-Sulaiman

Gabriel, the most loyal angel of Allah descended to earth with a heavenly *presence*. And entered the cave of Mount Hira to inspire the messenger with the poetic words of Allah's *essence*. I had embraced Muhammad's message from the very *start*. For his preachings of equality between male and female was something I already believed in my *heart*. How else would I have survived the constant *humiliation*? That society placed on me when I desired to be the first woman who could read and write in the Arab *nation*.

Nevertheless I managed to persevere and eventually I had reached my *goal*. No longer could anyone in Arabia say that a woman was unable to narrate a *scroll*. I often understood the teachings of ìsláäm better than the male *fool*. For I was a regular teacher in Al-Arqam's *school*. And what the women learned from me they shared with their men so they would no longer feel like a complete *tool*.

After Khadija and her neighbour I became the third female **Sahaba**, **Companion** to the messenger's *vision*. My specialty was practicing Ruqiyah, a traditional folk medicine that nurtures both body and mind with spiritual *precision*.

Umm-Sulaiman I Al-Shefaa Bint Abdullah

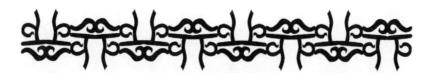

32

Al-Shefaa I The Healer
580 - 642 J

33

Umar Ibn Al-Khattab I Khattabo

What a traumatising time this was for *me*, I had publicly persecuted the first converts for all the world to *see*. But when alone I would cry my eyes out for all the suffering I caused *thee*. Every day I consume more and more *booze*, hoping it would take me away from Muhammad as if he were a mere poetic *snooze*. But the idea itself had set it roots in our meccan *society*, it seems as though some idols of the Ka´aba converted to his cause and therefore chose *piety*. Then, two waves of Muslims emigrated to Abyssinia where the Negus ruled with little to no *anxiety*.

I simply couldn't do this *anymore*, if I kept it up any longer I would drink myself to an untimely end without settling the *score*. I had chosen then and there to walk up to Muhammad's residence without *wait*. And assassinate him to set the quraishi record *straight*. On my way I came across my dearest friend Nua'im right in front of the Ka'aba's *gate*.

He had secretly converted without telling *anyone*, I replied by tellling him about my plan to make Muhammad's quest come *undone*. And he simply told me to go and visit my sister's residence first before I had my brazen *fun*.

Khattabo I Umar Ibn Al-Khattab

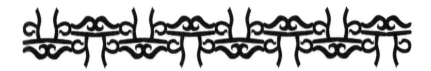

Al-Shefaa Bint Abdullah I Umm-Sulaiman

I remember the time when Khattabo's sister came to visit me for Ruqiyah as if it were *yesterday*. She and her husband suddenly heard him knocking on their doorstep in the most violent *way*. Upon hearing their recitation of the Quran he had gone completely *mad*. He threatened to kill them himself and when she refuted his threats he struck her down as if he were his abusive *dad*. After seeing the bloody damage he had done to her face he felt really *bad*.

So he helped her up and asked her if he could read the scroll that she dropped on the *floor*. But she made him wash up first since he had struck her in a manner of *gore*. At first he refused but soon after he gave *in*. Washing the evil deeds away while regretting his *sin*. Upon reading the verses his body started to shiver and streams of tears started dripping down from his *chin*. The next day he converted and protected the Muslims as we finally got a *win*.

And now we had suffered two devastating losses that left the messenger's heart *broken*. My services were required more than ever for I was the one to inspire the *outspoken*. It's time to build our unity may it forever remain *unbroken*.

Umm-Sulaiman I Al-Shefaa Bint Abdullah

Al-Shefaa I The Healer
580 - 642 J

35

Umar Ibn Al-Khattab I Khattabo

Even though I had become a devout servant to Muhammad, the final messenger of Allah the *divine*. I was still a fearless brute who would never fear the quraishi persecution for I no longer wore a *shrine*. I had cleansed my body from all nourishments that Allah deemed impermissable including my previously favorite *wine* cooked *swine*. For I am now no longer a victim to sinful *habits*. All idolatrous men that dared to deny a Muslim's right to pray would find themselves slaughtered like *rabbits*.

I had chosen not to pursue the others in their journey to Yathrib during the *night*. For I had desired a public exit in broad *daylight*. "Anyone who wants to widow his wife and orphan his children should cross me there behind that *cliff*." That was the challenge I yelled out in one loud vocal *riff*. Of course no one dared to even move as my fearless words had made them all stand scared and *stiff*.

In the beginning I wanted to wait until Taliba had finished his *quest*. But seeing the growth in him made me believe he could handle the *test*. Upon arriving I met Muhammad and asked him to install a brotherhood of the *blessed*.

Khattabo I Umar Ibn Al-Khattab

Al-Shefaa Bint Abdullah I Umm-Sulaiman

Upon arriving in Yathrib Khattabo suggested to Muhammad that he should install a brotherhood of *diversity*. Which consisted mostly of one meccan and one yathribi to undo the sectarian *perversity*. A unison of brothers from a different land who shared both faith and *heart*. Upon hearing this idea the women wished to do so as well from the very *start*. As in my mind both men and women were as equal as the tooth of a *comb*. Muhammad agreed to our request and I was paired with Rufaida who was a surgeon, nurse and social worker with restless healing *syndrome*.

At first the vast differences between our healing styles had caused quite a *schism*. But we learned to bridge that gap as we were both building the path to our very own *ism*. If we were to stand against each other both of us would have failed to succeed in our *mission*. That was the main reason why we chose to inspire the young ones to value *partition*.

When the first battle arrived Rufaida and I were glued together as one solid *core*. Leading the example so the women could inspire their soldiers to fight *more*. A landslide victory in which the Quraish had refused an *encore*.

Umm-Sulaiman I Al-Shefaa Bint Abdullah

Al-Shefaa I The Healer
580 - 642 J

37

Umar Ibn Al-Khattab I Khattabo

My cousin to thee I say *congrats* for you were the one who truly routed us as *rats*. But if Muhammad's cries had been *obeyed*, my cowardly brethren would have never been *afraid*. O how they ran like chickens while abandoning their *crusade*. And not too long ago they swore an oath to leave not a single man *dismayed*. In reality we had only ourselves to blame for this failing *escapade*.

When we were routed rumors had risen of Muhammad's *death*. But I knew the real martyr was Hamza who never anticipated Wahshy's spear to be the cause of his final *breath*. Muhammad was still amongst the living of that I was aware with all my *heart*. Since his most loyal knight was also my brother in faith and he would never allow the messenger's dream to fall *apart*. He told me before the battle that we would lose as he could hear our side brag about their upcoming victory before the battle was to *start*.

So we came up with a contingency plan known just between us *two*. If we were losing he'd lead Muhammad to the nearest mountain alongside his fearless *crew*. Then he'd screech his lungs out until I would come *through*.

Khattabo I Umar Ibn Al-Khattab

Al-Shefaa Bint Abdullah I Umm-Sulaiman

A siege by the Quraish who were aided by both Banu Nadir
and Qaynuqa two jewish factions that we had *expelled*.
When the oath they swore to honor Medina's constitution
was no longer *upheld*. Even though I could never prove it
I knew Ibn-Salul was behind this surprise *attack*. For he
possessed a scheming slipperyness that would never light
up until we would suffer from a destructive *crack*. My in-
stincts were never wrong and they clearly told me that he
was always conspiring behind the messenger's *back*.

Luckily a bunch of horseriders from the autonomous Banu
Khuza'a warned us of their *plot*. The warning left most
of our soldiers completely *distraught*. But by the grace of
Allah the Persian came up with the idea to dig trenches by
using his free *thought*. It was a very harsh winter condition
that made all sides suffer from the *cold*. But Rufaida and
I were able to heal our champions so they could forever
remain *bold*. After 27 days the Quraish gave up their *hold*.

A battle that was won by the use of both wit and *sugges-
tion*. Since that very moment every tribe in Arabia started
to ridicule the quraishi power structure without *question*.

Umm-Sulaiman I Al-Shefaa Bint Abdullah

38

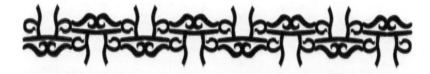

39

Umar Ibn Al-Khattab I Khattabo

In all honesty I knew the Quraish were going to oppose our pilgrimage without *question*. Since they had not yet overcome their loss in the battle of wits and *suggestion*. While everyone marched with confidence in their *eyes*. I chose to remain indifferent as I preferred the result of this journey to remain a *surprise*. As soon as Uthman had entered the convoy I knew they would not let him *leave*. For I had been blessed with a mind no man could successfully *deceive*.

Muhammad decided then and there to gather us under the Hudaybiyyah tree and form a pledge that would make the quraishi fear *increase*. It worked and when Uthman returned alongside Suhayl I knew there would be a chance for true *peace*. As both parties truly were in the direst of need to allow the tribalist tensions to temporarily *cease*.

For the pool of martyrdom continually filled on both *sides*. That is why they had sent their sole narrator to safely secure both our *divides*. I remember when Ali stood firm in his decision not to change the messenger's *title*. Even when we were at risk of losing this peacy treaty so *vital*. But Muhammad always *chose* to rise above such *lows*.

Khattabo I Umar Ibn Al-Khattab

Al-Shefaa Bint Abdullah I Umm-Sulaiman

Subhanallah, Allah Is Perfect for we were granted the opportunity to conquer Mecca without *wait*. After the quraishi allies had slaughtered some of our own in a vile attack of *hate*. The son of war pleaded with the messenger to accept his reparational blood *money*. But Muhammad refused out of hand for he found the gruesome attack anything but *funny*. He would march for Mecca even if it meant the bees would stop producing their magical *honey*.

Alhamdulilah, Praise Be To Allah as we had managed to grow beyond *calculation*. Our entire army camped outside of Mecca waiting for the quraishi forfeit so that we may claim this land as our *foundation*. Soon it would become the purest place for a Muslim's *prostration*. Until the end of time pilgrims from all across the world would seek to visit this holy place of Muhammad's original *narration*.

Allahu Akbar, Allah Is Great without *doubt*, for Ali was bestowed with an exalted ability as he started to *sprout*. It was often said that most men were terrified to destroy the statues of the Ka'aba forever shaped like a *square*. But Ali was born in their presence so all deities should *beware*.

Umm-Sulaiman I Al-Shefaa Bint Abdullah

40

Bãnu House Of

Uthman the third Caliph of the Islamic *story*. Also known as the first convert who carried riches & *glory*. In a way you could see him as the one who refused to give up *territory*.

The problems of his rule are what truly launched the isms and skisms you see *today*. Leading many members of the Ummah to be led *astray*.

Àbd-Shams

This faction is explained from the viewpoint of him and Hind who lived under her father Utbah's *wing*. When she was younger an oracle told her she would give birth to a *king*.

This made her very happy considering all the luxuries that it would *bring*. No wonder she tried so hard to resist the messenger's lyrical *sting*.

41

Uthman Ibn-Affan I Affanu

My father named Affan was a merchant who would travel above and beyond to earn his *wealth*. When I was still a little boy he died while travelling abroad as he always struggled with his *health*. I was left with an inheritance that made me one of the richest kids of pagan *society*. But such a treasure always fueled my already high levels of *anxiety*. Which was often made even worse when I would try to drink away my *sobriety*. All the money I had inherited and it still couldn't fill the evergrowing void inside of me that was caused by my lack of *piety*.

Over time I learned the tools of the merchant trade all on my *own*. I grew so successful that I was often seen as my late father's *clone*. Wherever there was money to be *made*, I would seize the opportunity without needing someone else's *aid*. Then my dear friend Abu-Bakr had converted as I saw him join the others while they *prayed*. After a long and heavy discussion I ended up joining the *parade*.

Muhammad and I were first cousins but we never really talked to each other *before*. Even though both of our houses had developed from the same ancestral *core*.

Affanu I Uthman Ibn-Affan

Hind Bint Utbah I Umm-Muawiyah

At first I was wed to a man named Hafs under my father Utbah's *command*. The unofficial head of Banu Abd-Shams who sought to ally himself with the Makhzums by giving away my *hand*. The marriage didn't last as I was widowed when our child Aban was still young of *age*. Out of desperation I married his established older brother with skin wrinklier than a *sage*. One day he saw a man exit our manor and he publicly accused me of adultery in a state of *rage*. The news had very quickly reached my Father's *ear*.

Driven by panic he confronted me as my side of the story was what he wanted to *hear*. If the accusations were true he would make arrangements to have my husband *disappear*. If they were false he would bring a renowned oracle to brand me with a public verdict of the future *seer*.

I chose the latter and so he arranged a ceremony given by a beautiful soothsayer of the Banu Tamim *mass*. She confirmed my innocence and even stated that I was to birth a king of the highest *class*. I married my cousin after divorcing my husband the *ass*. My prophecy had to come true even if Muhammad's seeds had now grown into *grass*.

Umm-Muawiyah I Hind Bint Utbah

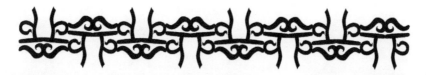

Uthman Ibn-Affan I Affanu

After I had converted the members of my house sought to make my life a living *hell*. Threatening to seize all of my assets since I had dared to *rebel*. They strongly opposed Muhammad's teachings as it was deemed bad for their *pockets*. That was the reason why they hired citizens to hurl stones at us as if they were *rockets*. If only they could listen to the poetic words that Muhammad would *spew*. It was in no way, shape or form different from the teachings that Allah hath chosen to bestow upon the original *Jew*.

The endless persecutions had become too much for both me and my *wife*. So I demanded Muhammad if I could gather the weakest of us to lead an Abyssinian *life*. I had already established the necessary contacts to continue my *trade*. So he agreed and allowed both me and his other cousin Jafar to lead the emigrants to a life where they would no longer feel threatened nor *afraid*.

There were 22 of us and at first we marched in the same *direction*. Then we reached a crossroads and split our group into both mine and Jafar's *section*. My group arrived first then Jafar's wave had entered this land of *protection*.

Affanu I Uthman Ibn-Affan

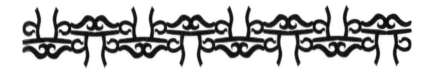

Hind Bint Utbah I Umm-Muawiyah

I couldn't have been happier when I found out that Khadija and Abu-Talib had *died*. And how overjoyed I was to find out that the messenger had uncontrollably *cried*. Now he no longer had a caretaker whom he could rely on for *guide*. But much to my dismay it wasn't traumatic enough for him to set his mission *aside*. As Ibn-Salul the aspiring head of Yathrib informed me that Mus'ab was making great *stride*. In converting influential citizens to undo the tireless yathribi divide. I never understood how such a young menace could suddenly develop a mouth so *wide*.

There was no way on earth that I would allow them to emigrate to Yathrib's *land*. As that would mean we no longer had the Muslims under our oppressive *command*. Over time it could make the number of believers *expand*. I wouldn't allow it so Muhammad had to die by my *hand*.

And so I developed a murder plot along with Umaya the fat *one*. We would raise the strongest soldier from every allied house including his own *son*. To enter Muhammad's residence and cut him in pieces so that all of this messianical madness could finally become *undone*.

Umm-Muawiyah I Hind Bint Utbah

45

Uthman Ibn-Affan I Affanu

Two years after we had settled in the Abyssinian's *land*, an envoy had sent word that the Quraish had accepted our religion and would allow it to *expand*. Therefore many of us chose to return back to the *homeland*. Upon arriving we realised that the envoy was sent as a *lie*. But I still decided to remain in Mecca with my messenger even if my family members would send me yet another *spy*.

We stayed until Muhammad ordered us to leave for Yathrib, the previously wartorn *city*. Apparently he had managed to cease the bloodshedding violence so *gritty*. I had brought all of my wealth with me as I was not keen on the idea of being someone else's *guest*. For I had already mapped out my entire future *quest*. To undo the trading monopoly that belonged to the city's Jewish *nest*. When I was finished both Arabs and Jews traded amongst each other without a single form of *protest*.

Then the time came for Ali and Fatima's wedding *feast*. He was not a merchant but rather a warrior that could slay any *beast*. He sold me his armor to pay for the dowry *fee*. But I gave it back as a wedding present much to his *glee*.

Affanu I Uthman Ibn-Affan

The Battle Of Badr
13/03/624 J

Hind Bint Utbah I Umm-Muawiyah

I publicly wept in the open desert after I processed the result of that badrian *battle*. My father, son, brother and uncle all slaughtered as if they were part of the *cattle*. I covered my face with the dusty sand to show everyone the pain within my *heart*. I continued doing so until my husband silenced me with promises of the vengeful *art*. He vowed that the following battle would result in the Muslim armies falling *apart*. I demanded he ask his ally Jubayr to bribe Wahshy his stone cold *slave*. As his impeccable aim could even hit a target hiding far away inside a *cave*.

Hamza I can't wait to see your lifeless body on the ground beware my *warning*. For hell hath no fury like a woman scorned while in *mourning*. I will cut out your liver and eat it in front of your *brothers*. As the hordes of people will consider me to be the avenger of all *mothers*.

I have already commenced writing my speech for the second drawing of *blood*. In which a barbaric river of red will most certainly *flood*. For now I'll simply incite my minions to spread the sentiments of my *hate*. For you never know which potential allies could be lurking behind the *gate*.

Umm-Muawiyah I Hind Bint Utbah

46

Al-Ameerah I The Princess
582 - 636 J

Uthman Ibn-Affan I Affanu

I had not participated in the first battle because I was caring for my sickly wife who had died ill in her *bed*. Then Muhammad hath chosen her younger sister for me to *wed*. She agreed rather quickly as her divorce had left her lonely and *unwed*. When the battle had begun, it seemed as though we had very quickly *won*. So a lot of us started to plunder the spoils of *war*. But we had no idea that the Quraish had a backup army waiting to *soar*.

I amongst many others had run *away*, unlike Ali and the rest that would rather fight until their lives would *decay*. The quraishi sentiment of victory was only further fueled by Hind the uncontrollable anger *breeder*. She would continually roar at the top of her lungs to cheer on her soldiers as if she were their true *leader*. At the end of the battle she victoriously turned herself to us and said:

"I have paid you back for the badrian *battle* in which my loved ones were slaughtered as if they were *cattle*. And a war that follows a war is always more *violent*, but vengeance was mine so for now I'll choose to remain *silent*. I say *thanks* to Wahshy who is now of the freed *ranks*."

Affanu I Uthman Ibn-Affan

Hind Bint Utbah I Umm-Muawiyah

Abu-Sufyan, I have never been more ashamed to be your *wife*. As you lost the battle that would solidify our polythe-ist *life*. We had raised ten thousand men with a few camels and 600 *horses*. And yet you still managed to lose against the three thousand unprepared Muslim *forces*. That Persian convert's idea to dig a trench really did sabotage your *precision*. As all of your previous advantages had gone far away from your *vision*. But at that point there was no more time left for you to stage an eventual *revision*.

You tried to get Banu Qurayza one of Yathrib's jewish factions to sack the Muslim defence from the *south*. But Muhammad quickly dissolved that strategy by using the diplomatic words that came out of his *mouth*. A true battle of wits in the form of a siege that lasted about 27 *days* and ended with the Muslims getting all the victorious *praise*.

As our team morale quickly fell after the trenches were *finished*, for any possibility of victory was truly *diminished*. Perhaps the time truly has come to settle the tensions in a manner of *peace*. Before it makes both of our already high body counts *increase*. It was time for a true *release*.

Umm-Muawiyah I Hind Bint Utbah

48

Uthman Ibn-Affan I Affanu

Ever since the Quraish lost the battle of wits and suggestion their feared reputation had come to a *halt*. Especially when Ali had slayed their champion using his angelic sword without *fault*. It was no wonder at all that they would try to disrupt our plans for pilgrimage by *default*.

Abu-bakr had sent me as an envoy to reason with the Quraish which was now under my house's *rule*. But the second we entered Mecca I knew they had played us as a *fool*. I was brought before Hind and her husband who wished to strike a *deal*. I was to revert back to my idolatrous ways so our house could finally *heal*. If I were to accept both of them would *kneel*, and they would also accept a quraishi rule based on my *appeal*. But I completely refused such a rebellious *ordeal*. For as a Muslim I believe that Muhammad was graced with Allah's *seal*.

When they had received word of the undying pledge of the Hudaybiyyah *tree*. They very quickly decided to undo the capturing of *me*. The narrator Suhayl and Muhammad drafted up a peace treaty much to everyone's *glee*. As peace always was the greatest way to trade *carefree*.

Affanu I Uthman Ibn-Affan

49

Hind Bint Utbah I Umm-Muawiyah

At first I was completely torn over my husband's decision to forfeit our *territory*. But after hearing my son's plea my heart replenished itself with a sense of *glory*. It appears as though there's a chance for me to rekindle my prophecy's *story*. **Allahu Akbar, Allah Is Great** for my islamic conversion was now no longer experienced as *mandatory*.

I shall bless Muhammad with gifts of every *kind*, so the citizens of Mecca would easier accept that which the messenger hath *defined*. It worked and for the first time in years the people of the Ka'aba shared an equal state of *mind*. From this day on everyone in Mecca would follow the final prophet sent by Allah the one and only *mastermind*.

I would march with the soldiers and encourage them with rage until my voice was no *more*. My soothsaying influence leaving its mark in every territorial conquest of *war*. All for my son to eventually set his predestined sights on the Muslim throne that every faction wished to *explore*.

I was finally happy for my prophecy was no longer *folklore*, all Muawiyah had to do now was establish the naval *corps*.

Umm-Muawiyah I Hind Bint Utbah

Bãnu House Of

A subdivision of the faction you've just *read*. Hind & Abu-Sufyan, parents of Muawiyah who eventually caused the Umayad dynasty to rapidly *spread*.

This is their origin story in which they try to *shred*. The messenger's lessons to keep their polytheism *alive*. Mixing worship and trade always served as their true *drive*.

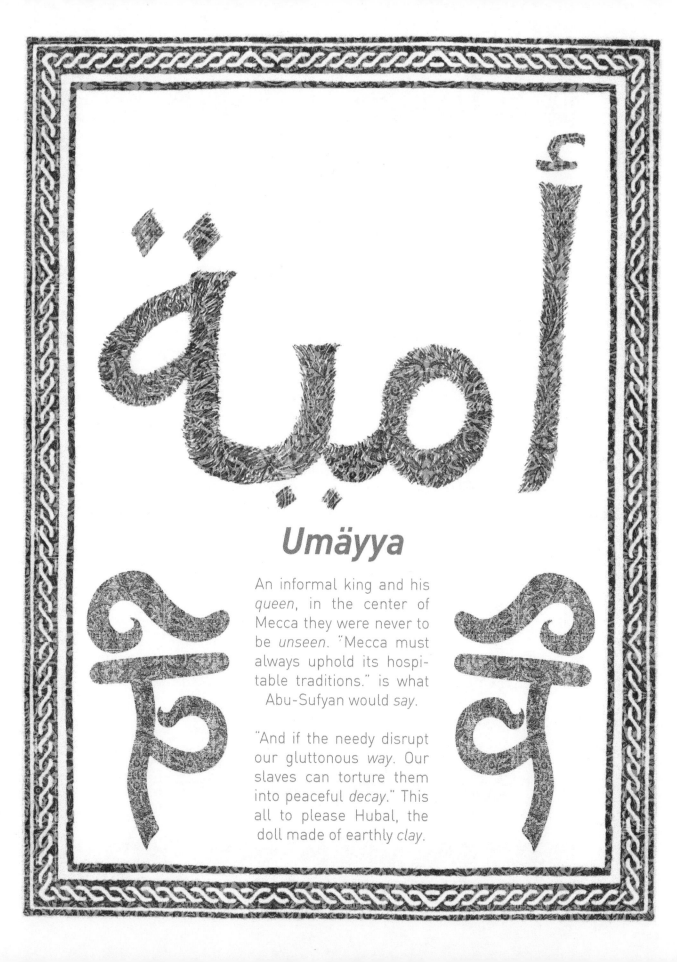

أُمَيَّة

Umäyya

An informal king and his *queen*, in the center of Mecca they were never to be *unseen*. "Mecca must always uphold its hospitable traditions." is what Abu-Sufyan would *say*.

"And if the needy disrupt our gluttonous *way*. Our slaves can torture them into peaceful *decay*." This all to please Hubal, the doll made of earthly *clay*.

Abu-Sufyan Ibn-Harb I Al-Sufyani

Ever since my cousin Hind was considered old enough
to be *wed*, I dreamt about our ceremony inside my *head*.
But back then I was a mere subject of her father Utbah's
command, so Hafs of the Makhzums was granted permis-
sion to ask for her *hand*. For I had not yet developed my
own piece of *land*. The marriage ended pretty quickly as he
died when his son Aban was still *young*. Then she married
his older brother who had a regular tendency to fall into
hysteria and publicly harm people with his *tongue*.

My radical jealousy simply couldn't take it *anymore*, I had
to sabotage their marriage to its very *core*. I entered their
home and lurked around until he was about to *arrive*. As
soon as he noticed my silhouette I climbed on my horse
and left in one fast *drive*. I knew that with his paranoid
temper their union would never be able to *survive*.

Then I immediately informed her father Utbah about this
scandal. He started to panic but I calmed him down by
assuring him that this was a situation we could *handle*.
I gave him two options on how to undo her *shame*. This
scheme of mine was formed in Al-'Uzza's loving *name*.

Al-Sufyani I Abu-Sufyan Ibn-Harb

51

Muawiyah Ibn Abi-Sufyan I Ibn-Sufyani

Abd Manaf Ibn Qusai was our common ancestor who fathered four *sons*. Two of them rose to prominence in quraishi society as the lucky *ones*. Their names were Abd-Shams & Hashim, brothers who shared a different *creed*. The eldest son Abd-Shams was always fond of the traditional values of merciless *greed*. Whereas Hashim the younger one preferred to share all of his wealth since the very idea of famine made his heart continually *bleed*.

Over time their houses were further established on the principal idea of mutual *understanding*. So when Muhammad first started preaching his angelic story to the masses we were still quite neutral in our *standing*. But all of our peaceful behavior went out the door when his teachings were slowly *expanding*. My parents would often take me to the Ka'aba and pray to the deities that their prophecy was not a *misunderstanding*. But their prayers were useless for Muhammad's character always remained *upstanding*.

From the very beginning I genuinely believed him to be the final prophet of *god*. The almighty Allah who would forever uphold the entire world and was anything but a *fraud*.

Ibn-Sufyani I Muawiyah Ibn Abi-Sufyan

52

Abu-Sufyan Ibn-Harb I Al-Sufyani

Hind and I were busy with building our dynasty so that it may spread without a chance to *divert*. Then Muhammad's mission clashed with our vision and there was a risk that our power might *invert*. Hind never stopped feeling betrayed after her brother Hudhayfa had *converted*. As in the public's eye she disowned him as a man of the *perverted*.

She would move mountains and split seas if it kept her idolatrous prophecy from being *deserted*. I on the other hand had no problem accepting that Allah hath created this *universe*. As the 360 deities were merely tools that I could use to learn and *disperse*. All so I can build trade relations with every Arabian tribe even the most *diverse*.

For our polytheism consists of both a religious and commercial *phase*. Abandoning the idols would mean that Mecca loses its power as a central hub of *praise*. Why would the pilgrims continue to travel all the way to our city of *amaze*? If Allah was present in every part of the world forever and *always*. Therefore I had to find something to make Muhammad abandon his *ways*. Even if it *meant* I had to make him our leader without my wife's *consent*.

Al-Sufyani I Abu-Sufyan Ibn-Harb

53

Muawiyah Ibn Abi-Sufyan I Ibn-Sufyani

After the death of Abu-Taleb the main *pillar*, my mother was preparing for Muhammad's slaughter by each house's strongest *killer*. Verily Muhammad did cry uncontrollably until his face became *pale*. But not long after he regained the will to further spread his prophetic *tale*. He took his beloved adopted son with him to Ta'if a place not far away from Mecca's *trail*. Hoping the citizens would accept his invitation to become Muslims and submit to Allah's *grail*.

In the beginning it seemed as though the current leaders were interested in his *vision*. But when they left the meeting all members of the common folk were instructed to hurl stones at them with *precision*. Men, women and children all together attacked to make their bodies bleed beyond *incision*. While the people were violently banishing the *two*, they ran for dear life as their bruises turned *blue*.

They eventually found refuge inside an orchard not far from Ta'if's *border*, the two were cared for by a Christian slave named Addas for it was his master's *order*. After a necessary resting time Zayd then went out to find someone who would bring them back into the meccan *disorder*.

Ibn-Sufyani I Muawiyah Ibn Abi-Sufyan

54

Abu-Sufyan Ibn-Harb I Al-Sufyani

At first I was against my wife's plot to slaughter Muhammad in his *bed*. But then Umaya The Obese managed to convince me so I gave them the go *ahead*. But much to everyone's surprise they found a sleeping Ali *instead*. That brave youth had pledged his soul to serve Allah's *plight*. He was willing to risk his life so that Muhammad and Abu-Bakr could leave for Yathrib during the *night*.

Sending out countless mercenaries resulted in failure as the two were no longer in *sight*. At the very least we could still plunder the belongings of the Muslims to prove we carried some degree of *might*. But in reality I considered myself a loser since I no longer had control over *them*. Now they all celebrated their independence making Muhammad their prophetic *gem*. Ibn-Salul informed me that he drafted up a *constitution*. That brought together all factions in an attempt to clear the city of tribalist *pollution*.

Yathrib was now no longer cursed with a tireless *division*. And Muhammad was their leader who possessed both power and *precision*. Deep down I couldn't help but wonder if he truly was the final messenger of Allah's *vision*.

Al-Sufyani I Abu-Sufyan Ibn-Harb

Ibn-Harb I Son Of War
560 - 650 J

Muawiyah Ibn Abi-Sufyan I Ibn-Sufyani

My mother wept as if her heart was broken beyond *repair*, but I myself was not that bothered for my elders had chosen their own *despair*. In reality the only thing that really irritated me was that Ali had defeated every enemy *fair* and *square*. He was the only one I couldn't stand especially after he managed to conceive the messenger's true *heir*. A not so sudden move that strengthened the Hashim's claim but of that fact every other house was already *aware*.

Jubayr Ibn-Mu'tim was the owner of Wahshy the only slave that brought the meccans to *scare*. A stone cold beast who would always execute his commands with *flair*. I asked my mother if Ali could be the target to *kill*, but my father silenced me as Muhammad's death was his preferred *will*. But Wahshy said that neither of them would *fall*, as their awareness during battle made his accuracy too *small*.

Hamza on the other *hand*, fought like a careless lion so his death would be the only executable *demand*. If only Ali would die at the next *battle* where my elders would be avenged for their slaughter as *cattle*. I could take his *place* as the exalted one blessed with Muhammad's *grace*.

Ibn-Sufyani I Muawiyah Ibn Abi-Sufyan

Hafid-Harb I Grandson Of War
602 - 680 J

Abu-Sufyan Ibn-Harb I Al-Sufyani

My wife had finally stopped mourning the *tide* and embraced her thirst for vengeance after the badrian battle was lost by our *side*. But I had to promise her that I would demand my friend Jubayr to use his slave Wahshy to restore her family's *pride*. If he were to kill Hamza at Ühud he'd find himself on the other *side* of the *divide*. As a man of the freed ranks no longer in need of a master's *guide*.

He had set his sights on him not long after the battle had *begun*. Wahshy hid behind a tree until Hamza's vigilence had come *undone*. As soon as he had a clear shot he threw his javelin straight into his heart but the battle was not yet *won*. Although I wasn't worried since **Al-Walid, The Loner** had joined us in our murderous *fun*. A man whose tactical ability and millitary command were equaled by *none*. In the past it was often said that his lance was a work of art that only the meccan deities could have *spun*.

57

He had routed the Muslims and many of them abandoned their *post*. Completely disregarding the pledge they had given to Muhammad as a *host*. After we won our women mutilated the dead bodies to praise the quraishi *ghost*.

Al-Sufyani I Abu-Sufyan Ibn-Harb

The Battle Of The Trench
Januari - Febuari 627 J

58

Muawiyah Ibn Abi-Sufyan I Ibn-Sufyani

Our side was still stuck inside the victorious *atmosphere*, after **Al-Walid, The Loner** had made our victory loud and *clear*. My mother was content with her *revenge* as she was now seen as the woman who would most certainly *avenge*. Not long after my parents were intrigued by the *proposition* of those who Muhammad exiled for their *suspicion*.

Banu Nadir and Qaynuqa the two disobeying factions who were exiled from Medina's *land*. The ones who were inspired by Ibn-Salul in his mission to overthrow Muhammad but things did not go as *planned*. The people wanted the two factions executed for their treason so very *grand*. But the hypocrite managed to convince them of an exile as he had never truly stopped playing by our quraishi *hand*.

After leaving the city they found refuge in Khaybar a Jewish residence with a magical oasis of beautiful *sand*. But Ibn-Salul kept fueling their resentment by sending provocative letters of *intent*. Even though he was the hypocrite who caused their previous *torment*. They travelled through all of Arabia to seek every tribe's fighting *consent*. A move that launched the battle in which I was also *present*.

Ibn-Sufyani I Muawiyah Ibn Abi-Sufyan

Hafid-Harb I Grandson Of War
602 - 680 J

A Hudaybiyyah Treaty
J 628 - 06 H

Abu-Sufyan Ibn-Harb I Al-Sufyani

After we had lost the battle of wits and suggestion we became all of Arabia's laughing *stock*. Losing visitors, trade relations and popularity all around the *clock*. If this were to continue we would no longer find the strength to tend to our *flock*. Everyday my wife and I would pray to the deities in the Ka'aba hoping they would answer our *knock*. But it had no effect since Muhammad's message was still far more solid than any kind of metaphorical *rock*.

Then one day we had received word that the Muslims were on their way to our *block*. I as the sole surviving leadership of Mecca had to stop them from entering our *shrine*. Even if Hind and I had to install a new leader from a different branch of the same *bloodline*. We offered Uthman everything he had always dreamed of but he refused our offer for reasons of the *divine*. Now Suhayl must draft up a treaty that both parties would feel comfortable to *sign*.

At least I managed to keep them away from entering Mecca this *year*. And with a peace treaty people would finally start enjoying the idolatrous *atmosphere*. I only hope it's not too late to salvage what's left of my *career*.

Al-Sufyani I Abu-Sufyan Ibn-Harb

59

Ibn-Harb I Son Of War
560 - 650 J

60

Muawiyah Ibn Abi-Sufyan I Ibn-Sufyani

The messenger's final conquest of Mecca was set up by my initial *contact*. For I knew the treaty would end when our allies would break their *pact*. Especially after I was the one who informed them that the autonomous Khuza'a had chosen to join Muhammad's side of the *contract*. I did it with complete and utter conviction since I already knew how they would *react*. It was only a matter of time now until the Khuza'a would find themselves violently *attacked*.

It took twelve days for the Muslim armies to reach our meccan *border*. After my father's initial request to pay for the damages was refused by the messenger's *order*. My mother wept uncontrollably upon hearing of their *arrival*. As she knew that conversion was imminent for her future *survival*. But fear not my mother for I had a feeling that you would accept the teachings of your previous *rival*.

Upon arriving in Mecca my father converted in front of Muhammad for everyone to *see*. I along with the other noblemen soon followed much to everyone's *glee*. After a nice little chat my father asked Muhammad if I could become one of his scribes so my mother would also *agree*.

Ibn-Sufyani I Muawiyah Ibn Abi-Sufyan

Bãnu House Of

Khalid Ibn Al-Walid nick-named The Sword Of Al-lah after the peace was *resigned*. Since his swords have been effective both for and against his *kind*.

Tactical ability and an in-genious millitary strategy unlike any *other*. All hail the warrior who fights un-til the very end but never forget the errors he made one after *another*.

Mákhzum

The other is the islamic
pharaoh, Abu-Jahl was
his Muslim *name*. Refut-
ing the prophet's words
so he'd maintain his in-
trest in the slavery *game*.

Father of both wisdom &
ignorance what a claim to
fame. But as hard as he
tried to break the mes-
senger's *poise*. Muham-
mad kept inspiring the
people to ignore his *noise*.

Khalid Ibn Al-Walid I Al-Makhzumi

Al-Walid, The Loner whose father was the leader of the Makhzums who excelled in matters of *warfare*. We were the greatest horsemen in all of Arabia forever riding with *flair*. From the very moment I was able to walk my father trained me to one day become his *heir*. Teaching me how to use the spear, bow and sword but the lance was my preferred weapon to bring people to *scare*.

I only knew two people whose friendships I would openly *declare*. My cousin Khattabo and **Al-Kadhaab, The Liar** who always broke the promises he made in *despair*. In our free time, the three of us were regulars in the city's wrestling *pits*. Me and my cousin were always the only ones left standing after grappling the competition to *bits*. One day he would be the champion, the next day I would take the *crown*, and the one who lost always slept with a *frown*.

As I matured my mind developed a severe obsession for tactical *insight*. It inspired me to work hard and achieve my goal to become a millitary commander that never lost a *fight*. Since victory was mine alone as worshipping deities in the form of idols never really brought me any *delight*.

Al-Makhzumi I Khalid Ibn Al-Walid

61

One Night At Mount Hira
610 J

62

Amr Ibn Hisham I Al-Firawn

Before Muhammad's message I was the one who had it *all*. For I was able make every form of ignorance seem as though it were wisdom by consuming excessive amounts of *alcohol*. I was also the metaphorical father of Khattabo whose toughness stood stronger than any *wall*. Together, our highly controlling arrogance would never *fall*. But now I found myself at risk of losing everything for reasons of the *banal*. As Muhammad was preaching his words of equality in an effort to bring forth our idolatrous *downfall*.

To me his words were mere **Bid'ah, Heresy** in the form of poetic *speech*. And he was not the only one who could listen to a DJïnn's mystical *screech*. I had to do anything in my power to make this supposed messenger seem as a mere *leech*. For I couldn't even begin to imadjïnn a world where his vision came *true*. A world where women could choose to marry a likeable suitor to her own point of *view*.

That was a dangerous idea for the ones who were as unattractive as *me*. Since it would make it impossible for us to get wed as a face like ours would bring no woman *glee*. I had to end this man before people listened to his *plea*.

Al-Firawn I Amr Ibn Hisham

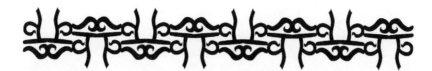

Abu Jahl I Father Of Ignorance
555 - 624 J

Khalid Ibn Al-Walid I Al-Makhzumi

As one of the richest & most powerful noblemen in Mecca my father staunchly opposed Muhammad's *mission*. If it weren't for Abu-Taleb I would have long been ordered to make his death come to *fruition*. But in all honesty I found myself rather intrigued by his messianical *presence*. And the poetic words he would preach to the idolatrous meccans truly carried an otherworldly *essence*.

But nevertheless I had a reputation to *uphold*, so me and my cousin used to persecute his followers until their loyalty would *unfold*. And when they migrated to Abyssinia I was the one who suggested that my dear friend Amr should bring them back in *chains*. For the ability to incite panic by telling lies runs through his *veins*. He was the only one who could possibly convince the Negus to banish them from his *plains*. But in the end even he failed as they were still allowed to live peacefully in Abyssinian *domains*.

Not long after that I had received word of the greatest plot twist so *far*. My cousin Khattabo had suddenly converted for reasons of the *bizarre*. He went to his sister's house and not long after he chose Muhammad to be his *star*.

Al-Makhzumi I Khalid Ibn Al-Walid

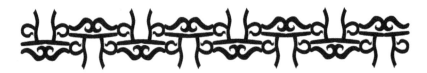

63

64

Amr Ibn Hisham I Al-Firawn

I worked day and night to undo my world of this messsenger's *plight*. But everything I tried backfired which resulted in him simply achieving more *might*. One day a group of twenty Abyssinian Christians converted to his *mission*. After they had heard his poetic recitation of the quranic words that talked about Allah's *submission*. I myself scolded them for their insolence since his dangerous ideas totally went against my love for idolatrous *tradition*.

So when the Hashimi boycott was installed I found myself overjowed with this *win*. For it made the Muslim bellies go hungry as we carelessly feasted on buckets of *sin*. But our boycott was short lived because of Mu'tim the father of Wahshy's *master*. A man who never wished to convert but still aided the suffering Muslims from even more *disaster*. If it weren't for *him*, the members of the exiled houses would have starved to death in a fate so cruel and *grim*.

Then I started plotting for an assasination attempt that would undo all of Muhammad's *madness*. But I knew the diplomatic Abu-Sufyan would never accept this plot of *sadness*. So I gave the idea to Hind much to her *gladness*.

Al-Firawn I Amr Ibn Hisham

Khalid Ibn Al-Walid I Al-Makhzumi

Oh cousin how your exit to Yathrib truly made me *laugh*. As no one dared oppose you since you would easily cut them in *half*. In all honesty I wanted to follow you but I still wasn't confident enough inside my *soul*. That's why I chose to remain here until I could achieve my true *goal*. Perhaps in the near future the three of us could come back together as a *whole*. Until that moment comes I shall simply resume to play my silent *role*.

Since the Quraish had seized the assets of the Muslims that *left*. Their merchant caravans found themselves at a constant risk of plunder and *theft*. Muhammad and his followers simply weren't going to *halt*. Until we safely return their assets back since we were at *fault*. But the quraishi kings had refused to do *so*. Resulting in a serious sentiment of retaliation that would forever *grow*.

After a series of caravan raids on both *sides*, actual blood was spilled which only stengthened the *divides*. The Quraish were preparing themselves for an easy *win*. But I did not join since I felt very uncomfortable in my *skin*. After I dreamt that the Muslims had destroyed the army of *sin*.

Al-Makhzumi I Khalid Ibn Al-Walid

65

Amr Ibn Hisham I Al-Firawn

Oh how my eyes turned completely *red* after it was discovered that Ali was sleeping in Muhammad's *bed*. I would've given the order to kill him for causing such a *bother*. But I couldn't go through with it for I shared a very deep friendship with his late *father*. So instead I went to Abu-Bakr's home and found Asma his eldest *daughter*. When she refused to spill the beans I hit her so hard it loosened three of her teeth and made her earring fall to the *floor*.

Then I left for the desert along with the Abd-Shams delegates who saw Muhammad as a cancerous *sore*. To see if we could find their whereabouts before they could enter a single yathribi *door*. We failed in this quest so I urged the leaders to seize any of the remaining Muslim assets without *wait*. Even if it meant they would start attacking our caravans to set the record the *straight*. If any blood was actually spilled we could finally declare a fight of *hate*.

And when the time came for battle I incited everyone to join us including Umaya The *Obese*. For our victory meant that Muhammad's mission would *cease*. But we lost and I was killed by a man who conveyed the message of *peace*.

Al-Firawn I Amr Ibn Hisham

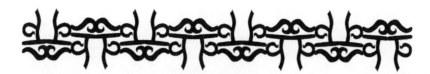

The Battle Of Ühud
23/03/625 J

Khalid Ibn Al-Walid I Al-Makhzumi

During the badrian battle my brother was captured rather *fast*. So I along with my other brother travelled to Yathrib to ransom him before he could be *harassed*. We climbed on to our horses and for days we marched through the desert so *vast*. Upon arriving in Yathrib we immediately demanded the release of our brother who was often seen as an *outcast*. Much to my surprise the Muslims agreed immediately and did exactly what we *asked*.

After we had peacefully freed our brother from his *chains*. He soon escaped and returned to pledge his life to Muhammad's *brains*. It was at that particular moment that I realised we were *tricked*. Since we payed a ransom fee for our brother who had already chosen his loyalty during this *conflict*. He was never truly captured as a prisoner of *war*, but rather pretending to be so their incomes could *soar*.

As soon as I realised this I chose to stand by the Quraish in their upcoming *attack*. For my tactical ability would make sure the Muslim armies suffer from a serious *crack*. As they would never expect to be assaulted in the *back*. I knew this was a battle in which they would feel my *smack*.

Al-Makhzumi I Khalid Ibn Al-Walid

Sayfullah I Sword Of Allah
585 - 642 J

67

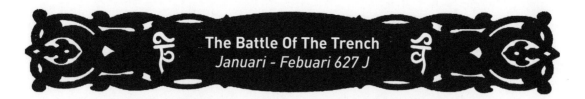

Abd Allah Ibn-Masud I Al-Tamimi

I was an early convert of the Banu Tamim, one of Arabia's largest factions located outside of the meccan *border*. So as a foreigner I was immediately let go of my protection by the late Abu-Jahl's *order*. One day he violently beat me up to instill me with numbing *fear*. But I was not bothered as I still chose to stand in front of the Ka'aba and loudly recite the quranic verses to every *ear*. I kept doing so even after my face was harshly bruised by those who refused to *hear*.

People saw me as the spiritual doppleganger to the messenger who was always accompanied by his loyal *knight*. It was almost as if our minds were shared especially when it came to the true meaning of the islamic *plight*. And when the badrian battle was *won*, I was the *one* who was allowed to chop off Abu-Jahl's head much to my *delight*. For that man truly was a vile reincarnation of the egyptian pharaoh who originally rejected Allah's eternal *light*.

And when we were warned about the upcoming legion of ten thousand *forces*. I immediately accepted the Persian's idea of digging trenches to disrupt their *horses*. In the *end* the Quraish suffered a second defeat without *pretend*.

Al-Tamimi I Abd Allah Ibn-Masud

Khalid Ibn Al-Walid I Al-Makhzumi

My brother sent me countless letters pleading for me to join their *side*. And about one year after the treaty was signed I no longer felt the need to *hide*. My conversion had sparked quite a bit of controversy in the *city*. Abu-Sufyan even threatened me with a deadly fate so *gritty*. But I wasn't worried as his threat went against the terms he *declared*. And fighting was also something for which I always felt *prepared*. So therefore I never ever felt *scared*.

As soon as I converted my dear friend Amr and his friend had joined as *well*. Then Muhammad immediately sent us into battle against a group of Ghassanid Arabs who carried a Byzantine *smell*. The battle of Mu'tah in which three people were chosen to *lead*. Zayd the beloved who died first in a manner of *creed*. Then Jafar lost both of his arms and died as the angels gave him wings *indeed*. And last but not least Ibn-Rawahah had also died by their *seed*.

Then the army was given the right to choose their new chain of *command*. I was the one they chose and the overpowered enemy fell by my *hand*. We killed thousands of their soldiers with our army that was *undermanned*.

Al-Makhzumi I Khalid Ibn Al-Walid

Abd Allah Ibn-Masud I Al-Tamimi

I couldn't believe we had conquered the meccan *city* as I heard Bilal calling us all to pray with his voice so raw and *gritty*. While doing so he stood on top of the Ka'aba forever shaped like a *square*. And we were all crying tears of joy for Muhammad's message no longer brought the meccan citizens to *scare*. As they all celebrated Ali's exalted destruction of the idols after our communal *prayer*.

It seemed as though it were only yesterday when I joined the other emigrants to the Abyssinian's *land*. After the endless persecutions by the quraishi noblemen made us all bury our head in the *sand*. And now I found myself inside the Ka'aba reminiscing about the battles of the *past*. I had participated in all of them with my sword that carried a fierce *blast*. But the one that haunted me the most was that of Mu'tah where all three of our commanders *passed*.

After they died the soldiers eventually elected Khalid to be the commander who led us to a *win*. But all he could do was safely escort us away from the Ghassanid's deadly *grin*. It was at that particular moment that he had proved himself to the Muslims as a man cleansed of his *sin*.

Al-Tamimi I Abd Allah Ibn-Masud

The Messenger's Double
594 - 653 J

Mecca

Ground zero of the Muslim *tales*. Back when the messenger's quests were often regarded as *fails*. But in the end he was still able to rightfully claim his meccan *return*.

And send the deities back to their hellfire *burn*. For Allah long since foretold the tables would *turn*. As the Muslim tales are of ancient divine *concern*.

مهاجر

Muhajir

In a literal definition the term means the one who emigrates from their *land*. But in the Muslim tales they were the true partners of this islamic history so incredibly *grand*.

The Ansar served as mere associates who aided in their true vision to fully *expand*. With a first *crack* leading to a schism where all sides chose to *attack*.

Dhiraar Bin Al-Azwar I Al-Mujahid

A highly skilled yet brazen warrior of the quraishi Bani Asad *side*. Me and my sister would often spend our days sparring with *pride*. As our differences often brought us to *collide*. We always lived very well in our *home*, and yet our parents never suffered from the idolatrous *syndrome*.

I remember our family's conversion as if it were *yesterday*. Muhammad preached the words of Allah to the quraishi merchants and warned us that we were being led *astray*. My parents joined the crowd in their laughs but in reality they agreed with the messenger *everyday*. One time Muhammad came to us in public and silently declared that he had dreamed a dream of *me*. That one day I would become a great warrior who would march into battle *carefree*.

When my parents heard of this they immediately converted as though it were a *sign*. Me and my sister followed as our hearts always supported Allah the *divine*. The one and only god whose mercy would forever *shine*. **Allahu-Akbar, Allah Is Great** an expression which was created in accordance with Muhammad's *design*. The final messenger to teach the lessons of Allah's eternal *shrine*.

Al-Mujahid I Dhiraar Bin Al-Azwar

71

Al-Arqam I Ibn-Abil-Arqam

Of the Banu Makhzum *faction*, I was the eighth convert noted in Abu Bakr's truthful list of *action*. When the messenger's teachings started to *spread*. The members of quraishi society harassed us to make our influence *dead*. But such highly sinful actions only enforced us *instead*.

Five years after the night at Mount Hira my house was selected to be our religion's first official school where we could all *learn*. The valuable lessons that would help us safely avoid the hellfire *burn*. As my residence contained a highly secret entrance that we could safely *screen*.

When Hamza and Umar had converted in the sixth year of our mission we reached a total of 40 devout men in the meccan *scene*. So we marched forth through the streets and shared our message to the quraishi *community*. We were met with insults and rocks as they tried to disrupt our *unity*. But our chain of bodies never broke as we were circling around Muhammad to preserve his *immunity*. I only hope Abu-Lahab suffers eternally from a fiery *afterlife*. For the blockades of bushes and branches that he would light on fire alongside his money hungry *wife*.

Ibn-Abil-Arqam I Al-Arqam

72

Amr Ibn Al-'As I Al-Kadhaab

A highly intelligent and shrewd nobleman belonging to the Banu Sahm of the Quraish *division*. At first I was all for the idea of ending the people that placed themselves under Muhammad's *supervision*. The quraishi leaders even convinced me to march for Abyssinia to make the Negus take back his *decision*.

As I arrived in the King's castle I saw the Muslims praying along side each *other*. I must admit I was fascinated by the entire moment as I witnessed them bowing down one after *another*. I couldn't wait to tell this to Khalid my *brother* belonging to a different tribal *mother*. It almost made me feel bad to complete my quest and bring them back in *chains*. I told the Negus a bold faced lie so he would immediately banish them from his *plains*. But sadly he never believed in disregarding reason from his *brains*.

He called them forward to recite some of the Quran's historical *spin*. And when Jafar was finished the Negus wept with tears dripping down from his *chin*. And the tears of his bishops soiling their wrinkled *skin*. He vowed to never harm the Muslims as they were all part of Allah's *kin*.

Al-Kadhaab I Amr Ibn Al-'As

Zayd Ibn-Harithah I Al-Habib

As a young boy I reached a certain age where my mother deemed me old enough to serve a *master*. And so we set out to meet with members of our tribe to employ me *faster*. But no one had foreseen the impending *disaster*. I was kidnapped by a bunch of horsemen of a rival *faction*. To then be sold into slavery at a shady marketplace for a mere sum of 400 dinars much to my *dissatisfaction*.

A man by the name of Hakim is the one who purchased *me*. All so I could be given away to his aunt Khadija as a gift of *glee*. I was kept in her possession until she gave me away to Muhammad as a wedding *prize*. Over time he grew so fond of me that I became the beloved one in his *eyes*.

One day I encountered someone of my tribe and asked him to pass on a message that would end my family's *cries*. Upon hearing this my father and brother immediately set out for Mecca to speak with Muhammad the *wise*. They offered to buy me out of his control and he in turn said that it was my *decision*. I chose to stay in Mecca for Muhammad was someone with a singular *vision*. May Khadija's afterlife be graced with all forms of heavenly *provision*.

Al-Habib I Zayd Ibn-Harithah

74

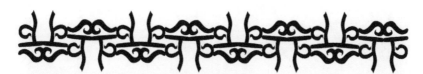

75

Abd Al-Uzza Ibn Abdul-Muttalib I Abu-Lahab

Of the Banu Hashim, an uncle to Muhammad and enemy to this *religion*. When he first started mumbling his teachings to our faction I cursed him for his *superstition*. I was also the very first individual to throw a rock aimed at his *face*. In response to his metaphorical words that my idolatrous mind deemed as a true *disgrace*.

He kept preaching lies and fairytales of equality & justice to preserve the hope of a *slave*. All of this divine inspiration supposedly acquired while shivering in Mount Hira's *cave*. In the eyes of Allah all men are as equal as the tooth of a *comb*. I asked him if Allah would ever make an exception for me as I have quite a superiority *syndrome*. He responded with a no and so I blew air into my two hands and wished that his religion would perish inside his *home*.

I did whatever I could to end Muhammad's quest before it could truly *start*. Following him around the entire city of Mecca whenever he would *depart*. When he spoke to the people I would publicly disregard him with all my *heart*. But now I am free of the Muslims as they've left the *city*. So I can go back to my seat at the quraishi *committee*.

Abu-Lahab I Abd Al-Uzza Ibn Abdul-Muttalib

Al-Abbas Ibn Abdul-Muttalib I Abu Abd Allah

Abu-Lahab's younger brother and also an uncle to Muhammad the man with a *mission*. At first I never agreed with his prophetic *admission*. But I always protected him unlike my older brother who abandoned us during the boycott in which we were without *provision*. Yet I still fought on the quraishi side in accordance with *tradition*.

I as a tall and big man was captured rather quickly by a small and frail one, Abu'l-Yasar was his *name*. When he brought me before Muhammad I felt something more than *shame*. Upon hearing Yasar explain the events he was apparently aided by a noble angel with impeccable *aim*. Muhammad allowed me to ransom myself and my son for little to no money at *all*. He said he'd expect me again soon in a way rather *banal*. Upon returning home I understood what he meant when I heard my wife Lubaba's *call*.

My older brother heard of the defeat and his eyes turned *red*, assaulting Abu Rafi for repeating what Muhammad had *said*. My wife then grabbed a rock and cracked open his *head*. The wound festered and he was left to die alone in his home as no one could bare his smell of the *dead*.

Abu Abd Allah I Al-Abbas Ibn Abdul-Muttalib

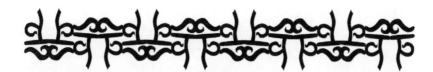

Hamza Ibn Abdul-Muttalib I Asad-ul-Jannah

The deadliest fighter of the Quraish who was yet to be *defeated*. I was only a few years old when the birth of my nephew Muhammad was *completed*. When he first started his quest I did not care to give him an *applause*. But then Abu-Jahl assaulted him and the lion within me rose up to fight for the messenger's *cause*. One day he even allowed me to see the angel Gabriel in an actual body *form*. I immediately passed out but I could still remember its magical foot that was shaped like a large emerald *platform*.

When I woke up it felt as though every last inch of doubt was gone from my *sight*. So I dedicated the rest of my life to serve Muhammad's religious *plight*. Our victory at the wells of Badr was the undying proof of our *might*.

But now here I lay wounded on the ground painfully awaiting my unavoidable *death*. That one and only spear thrown by Wahshy would serve as the cause of my final *breath*. I'm pretty sure The Princess is already joyfully dancing in circles around her *minions*. Let's just hope the Muslims will use this defeat as a lesson to never again disregard the messenger's rightly guided *opinions*.

Asad-ul-Jannah I Hamza Ibn Abdul-Muttalib

The Battle Of The Trench
Januari - Febuari 627 J

Salman Al-Farsi I Rouzbeh

I was the very first Persian that believed in Muhammad's *admission*. In the first sixteen years of my life becoming a Zoroastrian priest was my true *mission*. I eventually managed to become the guardian of a fire temple which was quite a well respected *position*. I guarded the temple for three years until I lost all of my *ambition*. But then I came accross a group of travelling Nestorian Christians and they convinced me enough to sign their religious *petition*.

My father however didn't agree so he locked me away in my *room*. But I still managed to escape and went with the Christians on their holy path away from the *doom*. I was given many different instructors to *learn*. But the last one really triggered my inner heart's *burn*. On his final day of life his eyes turned clear *white*. And he started mumbling a prophecy of a new and final prophet rising with his wisdom of *might*. And that my true destiny was to find this last prophet so I can pledge my soul to his undying *plight*.

I eventually did and truly proved my worth as we dug the trenches on my *suggestion*. It seems as though I've found my calling, **Allahu Akbar**, **Allah Is Great** without *question*.

Rouzbeh I Salman Al-Farsi

Al-Farsi I The Persian
568 - 657 J

Suhayl Ibn Amr I Al-Khateeb

A leading member of the Quraish and the general narrator of the meccan *identity*. The DJ'inn that inspired my words was one of absolute balance and *serenity*. As soon as Muhammad announced his prophethood I disregarded his *claim*. But even so I never sought to bring Muhammad's idea to *shame*. As I was a devout polytheist whose poetic prophecies made many revere my arbitrary *name*.

One day Muhammad and his men marched from yathrib to Mecca so their pilgrimage could be *completed*. But the quraishi leaders ordered a blockade to show their hearts as *undefeated*. As tensions continually arose at the border neither side *retreated*. So I was recruited to moderate the peace talks to keep anyone from feeling *mistreated*.

I drafted the entire treaty with the idea of building a long standing *peace*. However if either side violates it the rules of engagement would immediately *cease*. A treaty that was supposed to last for 10 years as a necessary *release*.
I even managed to get Muhammad to sign the treaty without using his prophetic *title*. As he truly was a man who believed reasonable thought to be more *vital*.

Al-Khateeb I Suhayl Ibn Amr

Abd Allah Ibn-Abbas I Al-Bahr

I was barely three years old when my mother Lubaba placed me in Muhammad's *care*. Since that moment we became inseparable from each other that I *swear*. From a very young age he would tutor me in regards to the Quran and the correct form of *prayer*. He would often ask Allah to teach me the true knowledge of this noble religion so that I may find myself free of the upcoming unbelieving *despair*.

Whenever he left for one of his *quests*, I'd go along with him despite my mother's fearful *protests*. As I knew that I was meant for great things at a very young *age*. That's why I always listened to the elderly men of life's final *stage*. For their words often shared wisdoms like that of a wise *sage*.

One day he lifted me up on his shoulders and I asked him how he managed to remain tolerant towards the unbelieving *kind*. He responded by saying that he would recite the quranic verse of the disbelievers before resting his *mind*. Since it brought him the necessary level of peace that was needed to bring the feuds to a *halt*. And it also helped him be merciful to the ones considered at *fault*. For even our conquest of the meccan territory was without *assault*.

Al-Bahr I Abd Allah Ibn-Abbas

80

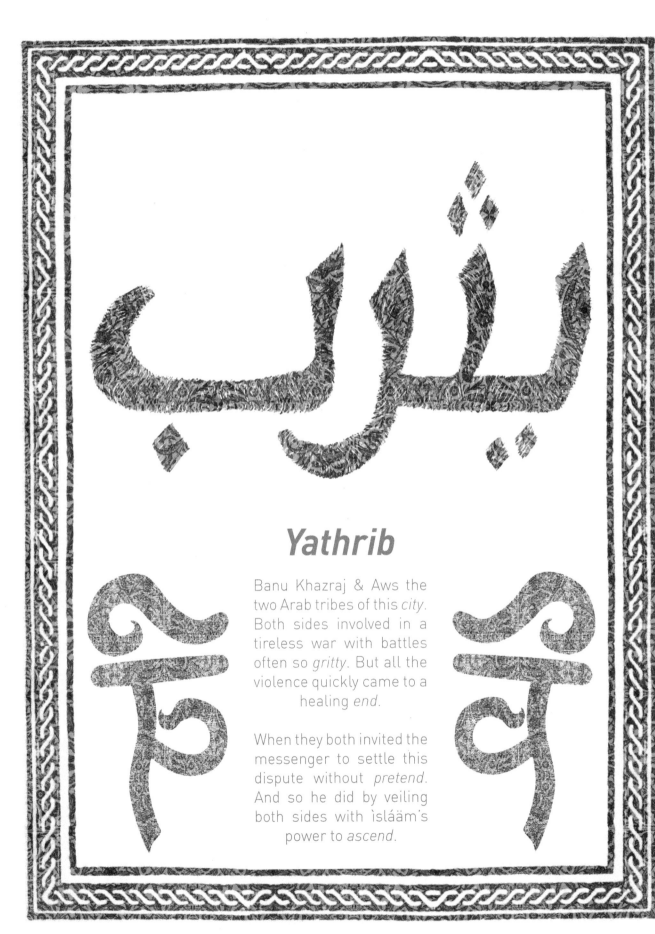

Yathrib

Banu Khazraj & Aws the
two Arab tribes of this *city*.
Both sides involved in a
tireless war with battles
often so *gritty*. But all the
violence quickly came to a
healing *end*.

When they both invited the
messenger to settle this
dispute without *pretend*.
And so he did by veiling
both sides with ìsláäm's
power to *ascend*.

Al-Madina

The seal of the messenger was veiled during the second pledge at Aqabah's mountain on a clear blue *night*. Where 75 pilgrims descended to give their **Bayah** to increase Muhammad's *might*.

The **Pledge** of war to advance the islamic *plight*. Among them only one female was Jewish, a woman who knew how to *fight*.

81

Sa'd Ibn Mu'adh I Al-Mukhles

After my brother was martyred I became the supreme chief of the Aws *tribe*. And as a leader useless shedding of blood was something to which I do not *subscribe*. I would convert rather immediately at the hands Mus'ab the grateful one without any form of political *bribe*.

For I fully adhere to the message of Muhammad's *submission*. In my entire life I have never heard of such a uniquely inspiring *mission*. Many yathribi's that converted came from every tribe within each *coalition*. Mus'ab really did prepare his quest to absolute *precision*. It was as if Allah had requested him especially to unite Yathrib's *division*.

Al-Ansar, The Associates of ìsláäm's birth and *rise*. Coming from all yathribi Banus to end the bloodshedding *demise*. By **Pledging** our **Bayah** to Muhammad the *wise*:

"Blood is blood and blood not to be paid *for* means you should not settle the *score*. So let us *agree* that I am of you as you are of *me*. And I swear a vow to wage war with those that fight against *thee*. And be at *peace* with the ones who allow the tribal tensions to *cease*."

Al-Mukhles I Sa'd Ibn Mu'adh

Mus'ab Ibn Umair I Al-Khayr

A young man from the Banu Abd-Al-Dar faction of the quraishian *alliance*. But my intellect far exceeded my youth as they often punished me for my intelligent *defiance*. At first I had to keep my conversion *hidden*, for in my household the messenger's teachings were completely *forbidden*. One day however an opponent of Muhammad saw me exit Al-Arqam's *school*. And he spread the news around town just like any other gossiping *fool*.

When my mother found out she locked me inside the *house*. So she could force me to recant my faith but I stayed silent as a *mouse*. When the messenger heard about this he instructed me to accompany Jafar on his *quest*. To Abyssinia the land ruled by king Negus who was most certainly *blessed*. Truly a devout and just ruler who kept the heart of Christianity in his *chest*.

And when Muhammad deemed it to be my moment to *shine*. I returned to Mecca with a courageous heart and solid *spine*. To eventually reach Yathrib so I can spread the teachings of Muhammad's *design*. Who received guidance through the angel Gabriel, a servant of Allah the *divine*.

Al-Khayr I Mus'ab Ibn Umair

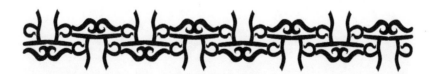

Al-Khayr I The Grateful
596 - 625 J

83

Jafar Ibn Abu-Talib I Al-Tayyar

A son of Abu Talib and an older brother of Allah's young lion *cub*. I lead the second wave of emigrants to the peaceful abyssinian *hub*. The first wave consisted of a mere silent *group*. But as I share blood ties with Muhammad king Negus and his servants often tried to *snoop*.

He was curious to find out why our religion had suffered such *backlash*. As he knew the Meccan sphere was filled with drunk merchants and *cash*. Surely they weren't scared to see their polytheism undergo a serious *crash?* I simply answered that before Muhammad's message we treated each other as complete and utter *trash*.

One day two quraishi delegates came to visit him bearing exquisite gifts as Negus always was a meccan *comrade*. Among the two was **Al-Kadhaab**, **The Liar** who mislead a verse of the Quran to make the king very *mad*.

After that the Muslims were summoned to answer this slandering lie so *bad*. All I had to do was recite the quranic verse that talked about mother Mary which made both the king and his bishops break down with tears of the *glad*.

Al-Tayyar I Jafar Ibn Abu-Talib

Umaya Ibn Khalaf I Abu-Safwan

A leading member of the Quraish and head of the Bani Jumah *division*. I would always participate with the pagan ceremonies as a personal religious *decision*. Distributing perfurmes inside the Ka'aba with a smile resembling that of Hubal the clay-doll carved to absolute *precision*.

I could care less about the other 359 as he was the only one I worshipped with all my *heart*. For he blessed me with an eagle's eye that could resist any black *art*. But I couldn't believe Bilal my best slave had succumbed to Muhammad's quranic *words*. Torturing him beyond reason did nothing to end his sole hymn of the *birds*. Even the Hashimi boycott failed to revert his loyalty back to *me*. As he was granted the title of Abu *Ali*, which was formed in response to Asadullah's personal *plea*.

Then came the swift conversion of my dear yathribi brother Abdu-Amr as a plot *twist*. But at least we were able to draft up a treaty so our strained bond could still *exist*. He guards my residence in Yathrib while I guard his in Mecca without risk of unfair *play*. But I made him use his orginal name for Abd Ar-Rahman is a religious title I refuse to *say*.

Abu-Safwan I Umaya Ibn Khalaf

84

85

Abd Allah Ibn-Ubay I Ibn-Salul

One of the leading members of Yathrib and unofficial head of the Khazraj *faction*. Before Muhammad usurped me I was supposed to take charge of *action*. Now I'm simply left to follow the Muslim herd much to my *dissatisfaction*.

Even though I insincerely gave my **Bayah** to *him*, I will always **Pledge** to sabotage his *hymn*. For in my heart I do not recognise the messenger's *call*. As I find the entire situation to be quite *banal*. A man who can neither read nor *write*, descending from Mount Hira with a mind so *bright*. On a mission to rekindle Abraham's monotheistic *light*. How on earth did this man accumulate such *might*?

I simply can't believe him to be better than *me*, there must be something else going on even the quraishians *agree*.

So therefore I vow to do anything in my power to disrupt the islamic *herd*. Forever sealing my fate as leader of **Al-Munafiqun**, **The Hypocrites** in the english *word*.

And If I fail I can still commit suicide inside my *manor*, for I prefer eternal hellfire to the messenger's pious *manner*.

Ibn-Salul I Abd Allah Ibn-Ubay

Abd Ar-Rahman Bin Awf I Abdu-Amr

The battle in which I had to face Umaya my quraishi *brother* from *another* tribal *mother*. I knew in my heart that both of us dreaded this particular *event*. That is why I captured him immediately after the three-man melee was *sent*. To save him from Bilal **Al-Habashi**, **The Abyssinian** former slave filled with *discontent*. Who sought to avenge his barbaric suffering at the hands of his ex-master's *torment*.

It was hours after the badrian battle was *won*, I tried to escort you away from the prisoners along with your *son*. But sadly we were spotted by the scorned slave himself as we were about to be out of *sight*. In a state of panic he scraped together a pack of Ansar as proof of his *might*.

I left your son behind to distract the group while I helped you to *escape*. But they killed him instantly to follow us through this harsh *landscape*. With your excessive body fat it didn't take long for them to *intercept*, I made you lie down and covered you with my vessel as you *wept*.

Bilal quickly backed away after seeing *me*, but the Ansar didn't care that they scarred my foot while slicing *thee*.

Abdu-Amr I Abd Ar-Rahman Bin Awf

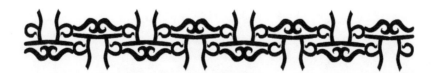

86

87

Nusaybay Bint Ka'ab I Umm-Amarah

A member of Banu Najjar, one of Yathrib's jewish *tribes*, I was one of two women that gave my **Bayah** in person to witness the messenger's *vibes*. My **Pledge** was without wait as I myself was without *doubt*. For the coming of a new and final prophet like Moses was long since talked *about*. By the previous books I adhered to before Allah inspired the messenger with the Quran's *sprout*.

I was only supposed to aid with the water *supplies*, but then I saw our soldiers directly disobey Muhammad's *cries*. Giving the Quraish an unforeseen leverage as we found ourselves on the losing *side*. So I grabbed hold of a sword and shield to march forth with defensive *stride*. Whenever the messenger turned his head to the left or *right*, he saw me defending him as if I were another *knight*. I took one small recess to gather my thoughts and let my son attempt to nurture the physical *pain*.

All so I could go back in for round two and defeat the horserider who finished my child's millitary *campaign*. I ran forward and stuck him in the *leg*, while he fell off his horse my brethren surely did crack his skull like an *egg*.

Umm-Amarah I Nusaybay Bint Ka'ab

Salman Al-Farsi I Rouzbeh

Ten thousand soldiers were on their way to our medinan *lands*, seeking to place all of our lives at their *hands*. Upon hearing of their arrival a lot of Muslims tried to bury their head in the *sands*. But I inspired myself off of Nusaybay and let my inner instincts *rule*. To dig the trenches that made the leader of the Quraish seem like a mere *fool*.

During the battle a dispute took place amongst the Mu-hajirs and Ansars regarding my *identity*. As I came up with the victorious idea both sides were fighting over me in a manner of *obscenity*. The Muhajirs of Mecca on one side and the Ansars of Yathrib on the other without *serenity*. Upon hearing this the messenger jokingly stepped forward and stated that I simply belonged to my very own *entity*.

Forever to be seen as neither one nor the other, some even started calling me **Abu Al-Kitabayn**, **Father Of Two Books** in the english *word*. In reference to my knowledge of both the Quran and the Bible but that title was *unpre-ferred*. Since I was also highly skilled in the Zoroastrian scriptures as a *third*. I quite enjoyed Asadullah's title of Luqman The Wise, as it was one I had rarely if ever *heard*.

Rouzbeh I Salman Al-Farsi

88

Rufaida Bint Sa'ad I Al-Aslamia

A female member of the Khazraj side, my father Sa'ad was a renowned medical *physician*. I grew up under his wing and he taught me everything I know about the healing *mission*. I converted rather quickly after hearing the messenger's belief in Allah's *submission*. As I myself never respected the idolatrous ways of polytheistic *superstition*. But I'd never deny Muhammad's words since they gave me the chance to prove I'm worthy of equal *commission*.

My practice was set up near Medina's newly built mosque right underneath it's largest *dome*. Receiving both the physically and mentally wounded as I was a surgeon, nurse and social worker with restless healing *syndrome*. I realised a great deal of complaints could be avoided if we were to envision some kind of travelling nursing *home*.

Because of the peace treaty I was able to take my idea to the builders to bring these medical care units to *life*. Then I walked up to Muhammad and demanded to join the battle of Khaybar in *strife*. He agreed and when he saw what the care units brought to the *table*. I was assigned a share of the winnings equal to the soldiers carrying a *sable*.

Al-Aslamia I Rufaida Bint Sa'ad

Bilal Ibn Rabah I Abu-Ali

The dark skinned former slave who answered Muhammad's call to *praise*. My mother was an Abyssinian princess in her younger *days*. But I was already marked for slavery in her pregnant *phase*. Serving Umaya The Obese in many different *ways*. Eventually I was secretly given a key to the Ka'aba's *shrine*. But I would never be seen as equal to them even though they let me drink from their *wine*. As they linked my hard work ethic to the dolls they perceived as *divine*. But I know better now than before as there is only **Ahad**, **One** *God* who is anything but a *fraud*.

Ahad, ahad, ahad was what I kept saying to distract myself from the *pain*. As my former master tried to whip me until it exploded my *brain*. No matter what he tried I never took the words of Allah in *vain*. After the whip came the scorching boulder that was placed on top of *me*. But even then I never stopped seeking refuge in Allah's merciful *glee*.

In the end it was all worth it though since I am now the sole minister of treasury in **Al-Madina**, **The** *City*. And also the first true **Muezzin**, who **Calls The People To Prayer** with a deeply resonant voice so raw and *gritty*.

Abu-Ali I Bilal Ibn Rabah

90

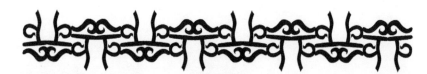

Muhammad | The Last Of His Kind

"Fatima, is the joy of my heart."
Muhammad

"No amount of guilt can change the past and no amount of worrying can change the future."
Umar - Khattabo

Rashidun | Rightly Guided

Fitna | Great Divide

"Cursed is the man who dies but
the evil done by him survives."
Abu Bakr - Siddiqi

"He who understands humanity
seeks solitude."
Ali - Taliba

Shi'ah | Succession By Blood

وضوء

"Solitude is better than
the society of evils."
Abu Bakr - Siddiqi

Bínt <small>Daughter Of</small>

Khattabo who tried to re-
marry Hafsa to Siddiqi or
Affanu but they both *re-
fused*. Causing the inner
eye of his ego to feel se-
verely *bruised*. So he went
to the messenger to solve
this *dispute*.

Muhammad married her
himself making their al-
liance *absolute*. While giv-
ing his daughter Kulthum
away to Affanu's *pursuit*.

Hafsa

Married to a man named Hudaifa until he died a few months after the badrian battle was *won*. After her waiting period she eventually married the messenger as another *one*.

She truly did struggle to accept her newfound *situation*. However in the end she was grateful for this *frustration* as it did help improve her *narration*.

Hafsa Bint Khattabo I Al-Asfaa

Muhammad I hope you can forgive *me* for the discomfort I caused *thee*. It was just too difficult to share *you* with the others as I often felt stuck inside a *queue*. But thankfully I was able to *grow*, after Al-Shefaa placed me under her wing and taught me everything that I need to *know*.

The messenger knew his final days with us were *near*, so he made arrangements to set up a final pilgrimage so the companions could *hear*. His farewell message as he would soon vanish from our *atmosphere*. A collection of his final words and acts of *praise*. Recorded for the next generations to follow the path until the last *days*. A necessary getaway after two false prophets already rose to *fame*. The third & final one waiting to pledge in Manat's *name*.

... Quran Sura 53: An-Najm / The Stars
19. So have you considered Al-Lat and Al-'Uzza?
20. And Manat, the third - the other one?

Al-Lat: Hubal's wife who loved to make *war soar*.
Al-'Uzza: Aphrodite of *sand* with loving might in *hand*.
Manat: Telling *fate* while her subjects did eagerly *await*.

Al-Asfaa I Hafsa Bint Khattabo

Hafsa Bint Al-Farooq
605 - 665 J

The Farewell Sermon
06/03/632 J

Abd Allah Ibn-Abbas I Al-Bahr

Upon finishing our pilgrimage Muhammad brought all of us together in one large desert *tent*. To deliver us his final message regarding the vast sea of islamic *content*:

"O Muslims, no prophet or apostle will come after *me* and no new faith will be bestowed upon *thee*. Always remember that one day Allah will make you answer for each and every *deed*. So make sure to never stray away from the path I set for you using my divine *creed*. A path of righteousness that goes against the principles of merciless *greed*. For all of the people originated from the same *line*, therefore an Arab has no superiority over a non-Arab by Allah's *design*. Nor does a non-Arab have any superiority over an Arab just as the black has zero superiority over the *white* and vice versa according to our true *plight*.

It's time that you learned to accept every Muslim is both sister and *brother* to one *another* for we were all loved by Khadija the greatest *mother*. Nothing that belongs to a fellow Muslim shall be legitimate to you unless it was freely given away with the utmost *will*. So do not do injustice to your fellows for it will surely cause the tensions to *spill*."

Al-Bahr I Abd Allah Ibn-Abbas

Al-Habr I The Professor
619 - 687 J

Fatima Bint Muhammad I Umm-Shi'ah

I don't care how many times you threaten to burn our house *down*. For my honest hard work was what truly supported my father's *crown*. There's no changing my mind I don't care how many of you *frown*. Never would I agree to give my **Bayah** to the untruthful *one*. For I only **Pledge** to Allah's lion who was seen by my father as his very own *son*. How quickly you have chosen to yet again *run*, from Muhammad's guidance all to achieve some powerful *fun*.

It seemed as though it was only *yesterday*, that we were back on our *way*, to **Al-Medina, The City** where Muhammad's rule would never *decay*. We had recently completed our pilgrimage in Mecca and during our long journey *back*. We stopped at a place called Ghadir Kumm that had a beautiful pond showing not a single *crack*. Right there in front of everybody Muhammed graced Ali as a **Mawla, Master** but it supposedly meant more than one *thing*.

As proven by the cursed ones who usurped our house to achieve their own royal *bling*. But mark my words for vengeance will only be *mine*. As my scorned hand would forever prove to make my destructive wrath *shine*.

Umm-Shi'ah I Fatima Bint Muhammad

93

Aisha Bint Siddiqi I Al-Shemia

Originally I was supposed to marry Jubayr, the son of Mu'tim who believed in human rights for *all*. But that plan ended when my father became Muslim as such a diverse union would cause quite a *cabal*. Then my father brought me before Khadija's *bed*. As she was waiting for one last embrace with Muhammad so she could belong to the *dead*. My father asked Khadija if my young hand could be Muhammad's to *wed*. She agreed and I was about twelve years old when my father gave away my beautiful *head*.

Of all the alliances he made through *marriage*, ours was the only one worthy of a *carriage*. But even *so*, our love could never *outgrow*, the unbreakable bond he had with Khadija who we all *know*. I tried my *best* to achieve that *quest* & in the end his last days were spent in my *console*.

In his final breath he began to shiver way beyond *control*. Proclaiming one last prophecy unwritten in any *scroll*:

"Beware those who wrong Fatima's *hand*. For you will forever feel her vengeance so *grand*. Especially if you abuse its power to martyr those who reject an unjust *command*."

Al-Shemia I Aisha Bint Siddiqi

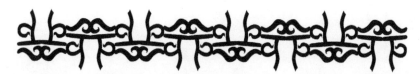

Aisha Bint As-Siddiq
613 - 678 J

94

Bilal Ibn Rabah I Abu-Ali

The very moment he found out Muhammad was *dead*, Khattabo wouldn't believe it as he continually shook his *head*. If anyone dared to confirm this news he would use his sword and choose that person's face to *behead*. Eventually Siddiqi calmed him down and brought the news to the public's *eye*. Then a group of us led by Ali went to bury Muhammad after his soul was spread throughout the *sky*.

Upon returning from our journey we heard that Siddiqi was granted the title of **Caliph, Successor** in the English *word*. After he, Khattabo and Ubaidah disrupted the secret **Shura, Council** of the Ansar who sought to fly away from the Muhajir's control as a freed *bird*. But the three usurpers were not willing to let that happen at *all*. So some of the Ansar suggested they accept Taliba's crowning at Ghadir Kumm before our unity suffers from a true *downfall*.

Eventually the Muhajirs managed to *win*, after Khattabo reawakened the previous Ansar tensions in a manner of *sin*. And when I refused to accept this sudden *decision*. He tried to use his power of manipulation with *precision*. By remembering *me* that I am *free* by the untruthful's *decree*.

Abu-Ali I Bilal Ibn Rabah

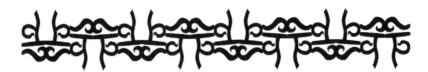

Abu-Ali I Al-Habashi
580 - 640 J

Ali Ibn Abi-Taleb I Taliba

When the messenger died I collected his body from Ai-sha's residence along with Ibn-Abbas and my two *sons*. We buried Muhammad in a wonderful Hashimi ceremony alongside the loyal *ones*. Among them were Abu-Ali and Salman Al-Farsi who the prophet saw as members of his own *house*. Even without a blood relation they were still accepted by Fatimah my hard working *spouse*. Talhah The Merchant along with Zubayr The Disciple were also *there*.

Upon returning from his funeral ceremony we discovered that Siddiqi usurped my title as *heir*. Fatima's face turned even redder than *blood*. As she gathered all of my loyal-ists inside our house even if their shoes were full of *mud*. When Khattabo was making threats in front of our *door*, Aisha climbed our fence and distracted me in a vile tactic of *war*. After he aggressively forced open the *lock* he failed to realise my pregnant wife also suffered from that *knock*.

A few days later she calmed down and demanded a repa-rational *pay*. But Siddiqi simply denied the miscarriage claims by once again twisting Muhammad's *way*. A few months later she *died* and her grave became mine to *hide*.

Taliba I Ali Ibn Abi-Taleb

Sajah Bint Al-Harith I Al-Tamima

I was the oracle who gave Hind the prophecy of an unborn *king*. For I truly saw a vision of her son sitting on a throne of absolute *bling*. And when Muhammad came along with his *mission*. I accepted his rule but never would I give up my powers of a *magician*. For I had mastered the sooth-saying prophecy in accordance with Manat's *tradition*.

A few months after Asadullah entered Mecca with the black *flag*, Aswad Al-Ansi became the first false prophet to undo his *gag*. He invaded South Arabia rather *swiftly*, but the Persian Muslim commander Feroz killed him rather *quickly*. A year later Tulayha swore in name of Al-Lat that he'd make sure to bring *war* to Medina's *door*. While Musaylimah publicly pleaded in name of Al-'Uzza to help him *find* a loving Khadija to give prophetic might to his *mind*.

After Muhammad's death everyone was waiting for the final false prophet to *rise*. And so I did by pledging in name of Manat whose prophecies travel throughout the Arabian *skies*. The people eagerly awaited my *premonitions* as I raised an army of 4.000 men from all *positions*. All hail Sajah the very first prophet of feminine *traditions*.

Al-Tamima I Sajah Bint Al-Harith

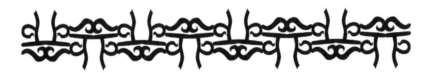

The Ridda Wars
632 - 633 J

Nusaybay Bint Ka'ab I Umm-Amarah

Back when I defeated the horserider by sticking him in the *leg*. The quraishis backed down after seeing his skull crack like an *egg*. So then I tried to get the scared horse to calm *down*. But I ended up knocked out after it kicked me in the *crown*. The wound took one year to *heal*, during that time I became a teacher whose experience was unable to *steal*. My brightest student was unable to be *seen*, as she wore an entire veil of which barely any woman was *keen*.

But nevertheless she was the one who successfully mastered the horse's *creed*. Khawla, the veiled warrior who I wished to wed to my youngest son Habib *indeed*. Until Musaylimah killed him in a manner of *hate*. After my son denied his self-made status as another prophet of the *great*. But I already knew when Muhammad made someone an envoy there was always a risk of meeting an untimely *fate*.

So when Tulayha's army laid siege to Medina I became a queen of the water *supplies*. Waiting until siddiqi declared war on Musaylimah and his wife Sajah to avenge my *cries*. After the declaration I signed up to defeat Musaylimah my very self but in the end Wahshy had beat me to his *demise*.

Umm-Amarah I Nusaybay Bint Ka'ab

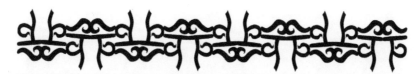

Nusaybay I Al-Mujahida
596 - 635 J

98

Wahshy Ibn-Harb I Abdu-Nawfal

When I walked up to Hamza's body now *dead*, I took my javelin and left the battle with a clear *head*. As the fight *finished* Hind's sorrow was also *diminished*. She made a necklace by cutting out pieces of Hamza's *face*. And gave it to me as a gift along with her husband's title oh the *disgrace*. To his honor after he gave her so much *space*.

I stayed in Mecca as a free man until the Muslims *arrived*, then I fled to Ta'if but the messenger's pious influence still *survived*. The Muslims were taking over all of Arabia's *land*. And I too wished to pledge my life to Muhammad's *command*. After I found out that all past sins would be *forgiven*, I walked up to Muhammad knowing that my execution could be a *given*. But he gracefully accepted and I out of respect made sure to avoid his eyesight at all *times*.

Then the messenger died and Musaylimah along with his oracle wife raised an army of *crimes*. I joined the Muslims in *war*, and we were able to climb their forts to open the *door*. As my fellows were killing the apostates without *wait*. I broke away to throw my javelin at Musaylimah standing by the *gate*. A bullseye hit thanks to Allah's *fate*.

Abdu-Nawfal I Wahshy Ibn-Harb

Wahshy I Ibn Harb
570 - 660 J

Uthman Ibn-Affan I Affanu

Muhammad always had a dream of our religion spreading all over the *place* without a single prejudice of *race*. Let alone the idea of culture manipulating religion for that to him was the truest *disgrace*. I never agreed with this but I never expressed my true opinion to anyone's *face*. And when Taliba found out that I gave Siddiqi my loyal *heart*. He wasn't surprised for he knew how I was from the *start*.

In the second year of his rule Siddiqi became *sick*, and in his time of dying nightmares of Fatima's hand appeared as a vengeful *trick*. Out of fear Ubaidah and Khattabo begged me to bring Taliba to Siddiqi's *home*. If he agreed to their request the succession would be his to *roam*. After hearing their proposal Taliba responded by clarifying his *creed*:

"From what I've heard all three of you expressed the will to *succeed*. So therefore I willingly subject to the rules that my late wife Fatima hath *decreed*. When you've had your final breath one of your sons can send for *me*. For I will never stray from the path that the messenger constructed for *thee*. I will bury you as I did Muhammad but Fatima's undetectable grave is not for a single one of you to *see*."

Affanu I Uthman Ibn-Affan

Ümm Mother Of

No one as she was never expecting a *child*. At first she was wed to Utaybah the man who rarely if ever *smiled*. But the messenger filed for divorce with immediate *effect*. As he deemed Utaybah to be a mere Iblisian *subject*.

In 02 AH she married Af-fanu *instead*. Widowed by Ruqiyah the older sister who died ill in her *bed*.

Külthum

It must be said that the messenger really did love his *kin*. While conducting Kulthum's funeral ceremony tears were dripping down from his *chin*.

How will he forgive Khattabo for the bloody *mess*. That gave Fatima a dangerous amount of *distress*. Causing the miscarriage that took away Muhsin's unborn bless.

Khawla Bint Al-Azwar I Al-Mujahida 2.0

I was a silent spirit that never really had ambition for *anything*. Until Nusaybah's bravery at Ühud made the warrior within me rise up and *sing*. I was her best student who managed to master the scared *horse*. While training all hours of the day to fully harvest my fighting *force*. And when my brother was captured I set forth my first *course*.

Sayfullah had made my twin a commander of his *group*, but he was always marching into battle carefree while leaving behind his *troop*. His capture was bound to happen *someday*. And so as Sayfullah and his rescue team were on their *way*. I left the other women behind and followed the men in their mission to cause *disarray*. I wore my full-face armor with a beautiful green shawl given by my brother as a *gift*. And when the battle began I marched forth to shock the Byzantine army with an attack so *swift*.

In accordance with my brother's *style*, I went into battle carefree and killed the byzantines as the armor hid my *smile*. I fought as if I were Sayfullah's magical *clone*. Slaughtering the enemies while remaining *unknown*. After the battle was won everyone wanted my face to be *shown*.

Al-Mujahida 2.0 I Khawla Bint Al-Azwar

101

The Veiled Warrior
599 - 640 J

Dhiraar Bin Al-Azwar I Al-Mujahid

The last war between the Byzantine Romans and the Sassanian Persians was fought in the fifth Hijri *year*. Back then we were still fighting the battle of wits and suggestion won by Salman the *dear*. And when Siddiqi succeeded the Muslim *rule*, he was immediately tested by the **Riddahs, Apostates** who sought to portray Muhammad as a *tool*. But in the end his strategy brought the repair of our *school*. So we set out for Syria to conquer Damascus the six-gated *city*. On the far western gate Ubaidah The Custodian reasoned with Thomas to prevent a battle so *gritty*.

Sayfullah on the other *hand* stormed through the far eastern gate and fought himself a way through the Byzantine *command*. I was adamant to make Muhammad's dream for me come *true*. So it was only a matter of time until I would find myself captured and feeling *blue*. I was rescued by the warrior in *veil* who turned out to be my twin *female*.

Since then we fought side by side in each *battle*. And when she was captured I slaughtered all of her wardens as if they were *cattle*. Then I made her *free* and she rose up to behead the Byzantine leader who abused her by the *tree*.

Al-Mujahid I Dhiraar Bin Al-Azwar

The Naked Warrior
599 - 640 J

Az-Zubayr Ibn Al-Awam I Al-Asadi

I was born into the Banu Asad clan as a nephew of Khadija the *great*. My mother Safiyah was Muhammad's aunt so therefore we were cousins by Allah's *fate*. I joined the Muslims rather quickly as Siddiqi listed me as the fifth male *adult*. Who embraced Muhammad's message and separated himself from the idolatrous *cult*. I fought boldly during Muhammad's entire *career* as my mother raised me to be a soldier by beating me until my eyes would *tear*.

Not long after the Hijra I married Siddiqi's eldest daughter Asma who was a woman with a brave *heart*. But I made her life miserable as my jealousy often resulted in decisions not so *smart*. I saw my horrible mother everytime I looked at her *face*, so when I was angry I often lashed out in a manner of *disgrace*. But by the will of Allah my mistakes made her bravery rise up with the fastest *pace*.

There was no way we could've won this battle without our women's empowering *words*. Whenever our soldiers would abandon the field they halted them with a warning of Gabriel's *birds*. The veiled warrior truly made the women's *wrath* help us win to build yet another new city's *path*.

Al-Asadi I Az-Zubayr Ibn Al-Awam

Zubayr The Disciple
594 - 656 J

Piruz Nahavandi I Abu-Lulu

The battle where our Persian Sassanian soldiers were defeated by Khattabo's fighters at the Eufrates *river*. I was captured rather easily by a Persian named Luqman The Wise whose presence made me *quiver*. He delivered me a message from a true heir seeking to avenge his *mother*. And if I aided him in his quest he'd free me as a true blood *brother*. If I felt Khattabo the leader of Muslims was unjust with *me*, I would be given a dagger to kill him for all to *see*.

After the battle was finished I was assigned to be Taliba's *subject*. But he refused me to honour the will of his late wife Fatima whose hand bore a truly vengeful *effect*. So then I was passed on to a man named Mughira who had a sneaky *disposition*. Constantly marrying and divorcing much younger women by abusing his cultural *position*. He was a shrewd man who abused the rules as a *tradition*, overtaxing me so my dreams would never come to *fruition*.

When I approached Khattabo about this he brushed me off with *ease*. As his sense of justice was only there when non-Persians were the ones to *please*. So I accepted the true heir's offer and avenged my fallen empire of *trees*.

Abu-Lulu I Piruz Nahavandi

Abu Ubaidah Ibn Al-Jarra I Al-Harithi

Of the Banu Harith, at the Shura Khattabo suggested I pledge for the **Caliph, Successor** *position*. But I refused and suggested that Siddiqi should make his dream come to *fruition*. From the very start he pledged to Muhammad's *mission*. And started convincing others to join us so he could note their names in his list of *acquisition*. So when he was plagued by nightmares of Fatima's *hand*, I was the one to suggest that Taliba should be next in *command*.

But he refused our offer rather *quickly* and this sealed all three of our fates rather *swiftly*. So Siddiqi named Khattabo as his successor while tears were dripping down from his *chin*. He gave him the assignment to lead with example and do whatever he could to find Fatima's grave so he could cleanse his *sin*. Every night Khattabo would roam through Medina to find her scorned *grave*, and every night he cried himself to sleep after failing his attempt so *brave*.

And when famine hit us *all*, I gave away food supply to ensure the poise of Medina's *wall*. Every evening he hosted an **Iftar, Dinner** to feed the starving bellies of the *poor*. For a starving child reminded him of Muhsin dying by the *door*.

Al-Harithi I Abu Ubaidah Ibn Al-Jarra

105

Muhammad Ibn-Maslamah I Al-Khazraji

A large, tall, black knight that uncontrollably *cried* when Muhammad *died* until Khattabo rose up to save my *hide*.

After the first two years of his rule he wanted to pay the reparations that would honor the messenger's *house*. I as a tax-collector told him that the price for such a reparation was a high quality slave either male or *spouse*. But Taliba refused and when asked why he chose to stay silent as a *mouse*. O how bad he wished to make amends but I told him he already was by ruling the kingdom as if justice was his all *along*. The people even chose to nickname him **Al-Farooq, The Distinguisher** between right and *wrong*.

And when Syria was hit by the plague of *wrath*, he went to Ubaidah who was the governor to save him from this deadly *path*. But he refused and died along with many *others*. Including the twin warriors who fought alongside each other as if they were two highly skilled *brothers*. And when the plague was *finished* Taliba's resentment was also *diminished*. As he gave away his daughter Umm-Kulthum's *hand* to our leader so *grand*. Khattabo was so *glad* that he ended up creating the Hijra calendar to honor the *nomad*.

Al-Khazraji I Muhammad Ibn-Maslamah

106

Al-Shefaa's Final Words
April 642 J

Al-Shefaa Bint Abdullah I Umm-Sulaiman

As much as i hoped to preserve our previous *unity*, I simply couldn't resist this once in a lifetime *opportunity*. When Siddiqi started a new empire I pledged without *wait*, since I believed he could truly undo the curse of the **Ridda, *Apostate***. If only Fatima would have accepted this as a sign of *fate*. We would've never suffered from her vengeful *hate*.

And when Khattabo made his horrible *error*, I had first condemned him for his act of *terror*. But when he succeeded the *rule*, it seemed as though he cleansed himself from all behaviours of a violent *fool*. Every night he searched for her grave while wearing a cloak of *disguise*. And the people he passed in the streets were always cursing his name while wishing upon him an untimely *demise*.

The people told stories of children starving to death in their *sleep*. Making him break down to a point where Muhsin's spirit haunted him as a *creep*. Every morning I healed his broken *soul* but now Hafsa must succeed that *goal*. How I must *say* that she has come the longest *way*. At first she was unable to do *anything*, now she can read, write and practice Ruqiyah after I placed her under my *wing*.

Umm-Sulaiman I Al-Shefaa Bint Abdullah

Layla I Al-Shefaa
580 - 642 J

Khalid Ibn Al-Walid I Al-Makhzumi

A few months before the meccan conquest Muhammad gave me the assignment to destroy Al-'Uzza's *shrine*. Located in Nakhla with mighty statues resembling a woman's love so *divine*. Ever since that desctruction my soul was taken over by a perverted love of *might*. So when the messenger told me to meet the Banu Jadhimah to preach our true *plight*. I did and the tribesmen gladly *accepted*.

But the pre-islamic tensions I shared with them made me forget that they were now *protected*. I ended up imprisoning some while slaughtering *others*. Even though they were now considered as my true *brothers*. When the news reached Muhammad's *ear*. His stomache turned upside down while his heart filled with *fear*. He raised his two hands to the *sky*. And pleaded with Allah that he should be freed from the consequences of this situation gone *awry*.

Ever since that moment I was given **Sayfullah** as a *name*. **The Sword Of Allah** as the messenger no longer felt that I was his to *claim*. I eventually quit the the army after my cousin Khattabo ordered me *to*. Because my men forgot that a victory only happens when Allah wills it to be *true*.

Al-Makhzumi I Khalid Ibn Al-Walid

108

Uthman Ibn-Affan I Affanu

When Siddiqi demanded that Khattabo succeed his short-lived *rule*. I was very reluctant to accept this considering his characteristics as a brazen *fool*. But I must admit that he proved me *wrong*, it was as if he was meant to govern us all *along*. Even though she originally condemned him for kicking Fatima's door as a *foe*. **Amir Al-Mu'Minin** was the title bestowed upon him by Al-Shefaa who died two years *ago*. **The Commander Of The Faithful** who ruled in accordance with justice instead of going with the *flow*.

Piruz the slave walked up to him and pleaded with him to speak with Mughira his *master*. For the high taxes that he put on his salary made his life a true *disaster*. So Khattabo informed himself about the *situation*. But he left it alone as Mughira was an established Arab who already reached the elder *station*. Piruz was mad beyond *reason*, but he was promised a higher salary if he built Khattabo a wonderful windmill that would lure visitors during every *season*.

So Piruz let out an angry *roar* and promised him that he would make sure to settle the *score*. The next *day* Khattabo woke up at dawn to *pray* and was killed in a violent *way*.

Affanu I Uthman Ibn-Affan

109

Ali Ibn Abi-Taleb I Taliba

I was truly surprised to *see*, the strong sense of justice in Khattabo's *decree*. If only my son Hasan would also *agree*. He could finally overcome the trauma of seeing his mother stuck between a door by a kick of the angriest *degree*. But he had his sights set on settling the score from the very *start*, doing whatever he could to avenge Umm-Fatima's broken *heart*. He was the one to tell Piruz to murder Khattabo without *doubt*, something that I knew nothing *about*.

In Medina's mosque he led the men to pray at *dawn*. And then Piruz suddenly appeared with his two-sided dagger already *drawn*. He stabbed Umar six times in the belly but the seventh hit right in the *naval* would prove to be *fatal*. The attack caused quite a public *uproar*, but he managed to escape after settling his *score*. He met up with my *son* but I never let him from my sight for he was my lucky *one*.

Piruz wanted to collect his *reward* but I wouldn't allow it for Hasan was the child I most *adored*. I snuck behind him and took the dagger from his *hand* then I stabbed him to make it seem like a suicidal *command*. I hugged my *child* and told him the truth would forever remain in the *wild*.

Taliba I Ali Ibn Abi-Taleb

110

Bínt Daughter Of

Al-Furafasi the Christian of Iraqi land founded in Khattabo's *region*. Offici-ally renamed **Kufa** after a decisive battle against the Byzantine Roman *legion*.

The battle of Yarmouk fought in the 14th hijri *year*. Around the same time an-other city was founded as part of Khattabo's *career*. **Basrah**, a hub of intellec-tual thought so very *clear*.

Nà'ila

Converted by Aisha The Brave as the two shared a very powerful *connection*. She married Affanu in 28 AH in a wonderful dress forever highlighting her skin *complexion*.

During the siege of their house she used her body for her husband's *protection*. But the rebels still managed to badger his face to bloody *perfection*.

Abd Allah Ibn Khattabo I Al-Farooq 2.0

"If Ubaidah The Custodian, my cousin Sayfullah or Salim The Free were still *alive*. I could nominate one of them to succeed me so our empire could further *thrive*. But now I am obliged to create a **Shura, Council** of *six*. To unanimously agree amongst them a new leader with no foul *tricks*. And if there's someone who's not in line with the *rest*. My son will stab a blade through that man's *chest*."

Talhah The Merchant was away for business so his vote only mattered if he had arrived in *time*. Whereas Zubayr The Disciple withdrew his candidacy in favor of Taliba who would most certainly fight all *crime*. Sa'd Ibn Abi-Waqqas however withdrew his candidacy in support of Affanu's *claim*. And both nominees said they would support the one who wins after Abd Ar-Rahman chooses a *name*.

In the end he chose Affanu to be the next *leader*, and the very first trial was settled by paying the damages done by my younger brother the blood *seeder*. Affanu offered to pay the reparations from his own pocket without *wait*. For he knew that Ubaidullah was not wealthy enough to repair his *fate*. May Allah protect us from all forms of upcoming *hate*.

Al-Farooq 2.0 I Abd Allah Ibn Khattabo

Abd Allah Ibn Al-Farooq
610 - 693 J

Abd Allah Ibn-Abbas I Al-Bahr

"Woe be upon those who think that my older son Abd Allah should succeed my *rule*. For such a thing goes against the very principles that I built for our *school*. Merit should always outweigh nepotism for *sure*. Just look at what I did when my younger son Ubaidullah followed the evil *lure*. By killing every Persian in his *sight*, including Piruz's daughter who had converted to the islamic *plight*. I demanded that he be caught and locked *away* until the next leader among you was chosen to judge Ubaidullah's unjust *way*."

Khattabo let me just say this from the *jump*, for you have evolved far beyond your previous ways of a *chump*. At first I hated you for what you had *done*, for Umm-Fatima's hand raised me as well even though I was always less than *fun*. But as a successor you always let me have a seat in your council table without using my youth as a reason to *shun*. As Muhammad clearly stated in a promise that I was the *one* who made sure that the battle of ignorance was *won*.

Taliba was the only juror who suggested Ubaidullah's execution for this vile act anything but *funny*. However the others all suggested he be forced to pay blood *money*.

Al-Bahr I Abd Allah Ibn-Abbas

113

Muawiyah Ibn Abi-Sufyan I Al Sufyani

"Under both Siddiqi and Khattabo's *rule*, I developed a naval corps to stop the Byzantine harrassment by the sea and make them look like a *fool*. Then I was made governor of Syria to make it great *again*. So I urge you to follow my council for I only seek to bring glory to both of our houses so *when*. You *see* something dubious done by *me*, do not question it for I only seek to aid the ruler that is *thee*."

Oh cousin how easy it was to manipulate you without *wait*. For I had convinced you to invest your entire wealth into this *Caliphate*. The unjust rulings were there from the *start*. But so long as the money kept flowing the people preferred to practice the indifferent *art*. Then the wells of cash started to go *dry*, and your supporters quickly started complaining about you as an *ally*. But no matter what they said you always sat there with your head lifted to the *sky*.

When Khattabo ruled he always kept me in a tight *frame*. And every time I ran wild he made sure that I alone would be the one to *blame*. But you were just a silent little lamb who unforeseenly rose to *fame*. And when you fired **Al-Kadhaab, The Liar** as governor he really hated your *claim*.

Al Sufyani I Muawiyah Ibn Abi-Sufyan

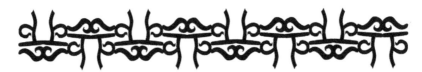

Abd Ar-Rahman Bin Awf I Abdu-Amr

"When the votes were tied I had to unite the *division*. So I asked Taliba if he would follow the Quran, Sunnah and both Siddiqi and Khattabo's *vision*. And he replied that he would follow the first two with *precision*, but the last thing I suggested he would replace with his personal *decision*. And when I asked Affanu the same *thing*, he immediately agreed by saying yes to my request as if it were *nothing*."

But now I realised Affanu lied directly to my *face*, not only did he unfollow the way of Siddiqi and Khattabo's *grace*. He also disregarded the Sunnah in a manner of absolute *disgrace*. By changing the ways of our prayer and other things as Muhammad's legacy risked a permanent *erase*.

Back when the apostate battles were *finished*, 700 **Hafiz** lives were also *diminished*. **Keepers** who knew all of the quranic verses by *heart* & were able to recite them from finish to *start*. So Zayd ibn Thabit was ordered to recollect all of the verses in one *book*. And Affanu used that to make an official version to distribute it as a *handbook*. He then sent a copy to every governor and ordered them to burn all other forms of the Quran as if he were a hellfire *crook*.

Abdu-Amr I Abd Ar-Rahman Bin Awf

114

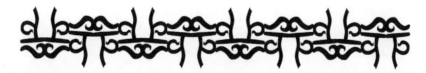

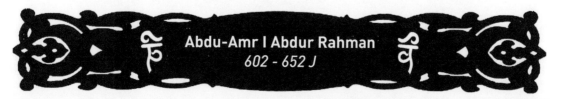

115

Aisha Bint Siddiqi I Al-Shemia

"How soon you have forgotten the **Sunnah** of the messenger *indeed*. The **Teachings** that go against the principles of corrupt and merciless *greed*. Here I stand carrying his shirt and sandals for his heart would surely *bleed*. If he saw how you destroyed the justice of his divine *creed*.
I urge you to listen to my council so you can take heed.
Of your failing rule inspired by those of the Iblisian *seed*."

In the first two Caliphates I was a highly valued consultant who made sure to uphold the duties of a societal *chain*. Then you came to power and it took me years to wiggle my way inside your *reign*. But the only job you had for me required tons of beauty and not even a little bit of *brain*.
I was to accompany your wife Na'ila in beautiful dresses and *shoes*. Sitting there with a mindless purpose while the ignorant men discussed their supposedly superior *views*.

How I had grown to despise you for the things you had *done*. We as women were so close to making sure the battle of inequality was *won*. You were the reason why I inspired the women to wear the *veil*. For there exists no greater duty than a woman blocking the gaze of a *male*.

Al-Shemia I Aisha Bint Siddiqi

When Nepotism Decrees
650 - 656 J

Ali Ibn Abi-Taleb I Taliba

"When Khattabo was the ruler of *men*, he would beat & scold Mu'awiyah for his insolence over and *again*. But you simply allowed him to roam *free*, giving him the chance to humiliate *thee*. How is it so hard for you to *see*, that his council is just an attempt to turn you against *me*. I'm simply advising you out of *fear*, for I think it won't be long until the people shall no longer *adhere*. To your *will* so be careful Affanu for you may become someone's target to *kill*. And I myself would truly hate to see the tensions *spill*."

Even though Aisha and I never really got *along*, I completely agreed with her plight that justice was the only side to which a ruler should *belong*. His half-brother Walid deserved to be punished by the verdict of *law*, but Affanu ignored the people as he was dumbed down by Mu'awiyah's *claw*. If I hadn't *done* what I did to protect my mistaken *son*. I might've been far angrier with Affanu the silent *one*.

But I *did* so therefore my honest opinion was forced to be *hid*. I gave my **Bayah** to his elder *face*, therefore I shall not undo my **Pledge** for Allah would deem it a *disgrace*. Hopefully the rebels don't turn out to be the victors of this *race*.

Taliba I Ali Ibn Abi-Taleb

116

Taliba I Asadullah
594 - 661 J

117

Muhammad Ibn Abi-Hudhayfa I Abdu-Affanu

"My father was Hind's brother who chose to convert without *wait*. And when he died while fighting Musaylimah the *apostate*. I was placed into your care since the others of our house already refused me in a manner of *hate*. I did everything I could to repay the *favor*, but you always subdued me by remembering me that you were my *lifesaver*. And when you came to *power* I was given not a single chance to prove that I was worthy of a place in your *tower*."

It was bad enough when he replaced **Al-Kadhaab, The Liar** with Sa'd Ibn Abi-Waqqas to rule Egypt the *land* where the pharaoh was lifted from his *command*. For Sa'd was only good at drinking *booze* and making his critics *bruise*. But things took a turn for the *worse* when Abd Allah Ibn-Saad ruled according to his corrupt mindset just like a *curse*, and a societal standard anything but *diverse*.

Two horrible examples and not once did he even think to nominate *me*. So I forged Aisha's signature and started a rebellion for everyone to *see*. Eventually I was able to launch a *coup*, as my forgery made sure the amount of rebels *grew* until it made me leader of the pyramid's *view*.

Abdu-Affanu I Muhammad Ibn Abi-Hudhayfa

Na'ila Bint Al-Furafisa I Al-Uthmaniya

"Husband I urge you to listen to their *plea*, for in my heart I believe you're being played by your cousin Marwan the *flea*. From the very moment he entered your *life*, his slippery behaviour was seen as suspicious by me, your *wife*. The rebels even wanted to cut off our water *supply*, but Taliba talked them out of it as a real good *guy*. If you gave up your crown perhaps the people would no longer look at you with a deadly *frown*. Please do not make me a *widow* for that was a fate that would render me unable to *grow*."

The scorned rebels gathered around our *house*, protesting your rule while you simply sat there as silent as a *mouse*. The rebels comprised of both Muhajirs and Ansars as one violent *bunch*. So you sent both Taliba and The Messenger's Knight to settle the tensions before someone throws a *punch*. They gave every complaint a listening *ear* and returned to you with a list of requests for you to *adhere*.

But your cousin was once again able to bend your *mind* by making you doubt the severity of the rebel *kind*. I'm just grateful Aisha's rebellion was a *lie*. Forged by the one that saw you as a guardian but you never saw him as an *ally*.

Al-Uthmaniya I Na'ila Bint Al-Furafisa

Marwan Ibn Al-Hakam I Al-Marwani

"Fear not Affanu for I was chosen to be your secretary for a *reason*. So I will make sure to dissolve the tensions before anyone decides to commit *treason*. Never will I show you what I plan to *do*, for as a true leader such information is not useful to *you*. We have grown to be very close you and *I*, that's the reason why you should never quit being my *ally*. Name me a mountain and I'll move it without *wait* for you were instructed by Allah's *fate*. *Tomorrow* you should give a sermon to warn everyone of future *sorrow*."

Affanu you must be the most gullable ruler I've ever *seen*. For every single one of my manipulations have been flagged by others as *obscene*. But you never really let me out of your *sight*, as the old age decreased quite a bit of your physical *might*. Giving me the opportunity to use my slipperyness and further tear down your ethical *plight*.

It seemed as though it was only yesterday that Muawiyah wrote to *me*. And shared the diabolical plan by Amr, the previous governor of Egypt to destroy *thee*. I forged your signature to send a letter that carried your *seal*. Telling the new governor that the rebel lives were his to *steal*.

Al-Marwani I Marwan Ibn Al-Hakam

Marwan I Al-Hakam
626 - 685 J

Muhammad Ibn-Maslamah I Al-Khazraji

"It was impossible to overlook the obvious *issue*, you have stained our valor to a point where it became unable to wipe it away with a *tissue*. The people wanted you to step down clear as *day*, for you've been the perfect example of a leader who allowed himself to be led *astray*. The rebels were loud & *clear*, it was time for you to step down and no longer rule over the islamic *sphere*. You've chosen me yet again to defend your cause without *wait*, but I refused to do so since you did not repair the sentiments of *hate*."

First you walked into the mosque and addressed everyone who rebelled against *you*. Using the words of Allah without ever even trying to think them *through*. For you were the very first example of an unjust *head*. Seeing how the rebels reacted to you made me believe you'd soon be *dead*.

Then they chose to return back to Egypt's *land*. While on their way they halted a suspicious looking caravan containing a letter with your seal of *command*. After reading it they went mad with *rage*, returning to your house to make sure you didn't die of old *age*. You denied writing it but still defended the vile secretary who had your mind in a *cage*.

Al-Khazraji I Muhammad Ibn-Maslamah

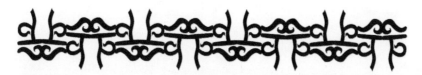

120

Ümm Mother Of

Hasan & Husayn followers of the Shi'ah *throne*. The true heirs who were never left *alone*. By the Kufa loyalists imadjinning a leader coming from one of their *own*.

As the **Ahl-Al-Bayt** is what the Shi'ahs are all *about*. Aiding **The People Of Muhammad's House** as they *sprout*. To make their claim without *doubt*.

Fátima

Verily hell hath no great-
er fury than a woman
scorned while in *mourn-
ing*. As she made Taliba
bury her without giving
the others fair *warning*.

How many nights Khat-
tabo spent searching for
her unmarked *grave*. But
he never found it as her
Qareen deemed his soul
unworthy to *save*. A **Djinn**
with an eerie sound *wave*.

Aisha Bint Siddiqi I Al-Shemia

"Aisha I couldn't believe my *eyes* when I saw three rebels entering our room as Affanu ignored my *cries*. He was reciting the Quran for all to *hear*, unafraid of his upcoming death so very *near*. I jumped on his body to save him from *harm*, but they pulled me away and looted all of my jewellery including my luckiest *charm*. They kept punching until it was impossible to remember his *face*. He had a dream the day before in which Muhammad warned him of his last resting *place*. I beg of you help me avenge this *disgrace*."

Na'ila as much as I love you I couldn't help but feel happy for your *pain*. Since the death of such a useless and unjust leader can only bring me *gain*. Affanu's dead body was rotting inside his house for three whole *days*, until a group of twelve took him to a burial ground so Allah could judge him for his *ways*. Taliba and his two sons were also *there*, they even stayed long enough to conduct his funeral *prayer*. But even in his death I felt unmoved by this *affair*.

For to me Affanu was not a just leader for *all*, but rather a ruler who made sure the Abd-Shams house would never *fall*. Hopefully the people will now choose my name to *call*.

Al-Shemia I Aisha Bint Siddiqi

Taliba, First Of The Shi'ahs
August 656 J

Salman Al-Farsi I Rouzbeh

"Luqman, let me start by telling you that I am not *mad*. For you had your own reasons of killing Khattabo who you saw as *bad*. The only thing I would've wished was that you kept my son Hasan out of the *equation*. But what's done is done so let us now overlook the entire *occasion*. As now I am in dire need of your powers of *persuasion*. Since I've been forced to accept the succession to Affanu's *rule*. So help me guide the Muslims back to their original *school*. It's the only way for us to repent after hiding the murder *tool*."

After Affanu's death the rebels stayed in Medina and demanded Taliba to take the *crown*. At first he immediately refused but then he was forced to accept after the rebels had threatened to burn all of Medina *down*. So he came to me to forgive me for what I had *done*. But I never had the strength to tell him that the entire idea came from his very own *son*. I told him that I had fallen *ill* but for as long as I was among the living I would use my persuasion *skill*.

As we all knew that Affanu's death would make everyone's sense of justice rise higher than the *skies*. But in the end they would all prove to be selfish endeavours in *disguise*.

Rouzbeh I Salman Al-Farsi

Luqman The Wise
568 - 657 J

123

Muhammad Ibn-Maslamah I Al-Khazraji

"O knight of *mine*, everyday you are by my side to make my safety *shine*. Even at this loss of Ũhud you were still the one who stayed closest to *me*. So therefore I grant you this sword for not a single soul to *see*. If you ever witness the Muslims enticed once again by merciless *greed*. It will result in a **Fitna** that would go against my divine *creed*. **The Great Divide** in which all Muslims decide to kill each other's *seed*. When that day is *here* I want you to climb Ũhud's mountain and break this sword I once held *dear*."

It truly pains me to say that day has *come*, for everyone seems to be using Affanu's death as a reason to *succumb*. To personal endeavours as Aisha, Talhah and Zubayr joined Marwan's unholy *quest*. To launch a rebellion against Taliba as they denied him to be the *best*. I myself also refrained from pledging to Taliba's *rule*. But I would never rebel against someone who wasn't even given the chance to prove himself a *fool*. I along with Khattabo's older son refrained from this rebellion anything but *cool*.

Especially when we realised the rebellion was funded by Marwan who stole *cash* from our treasury what a *trash*.

Al-Khazraji I Muhammad Ibn-Maslamah

Marwan Ibn Al-Hakam I Al-Marwani

"My cousin for you I have a *quest*, in which you have to set the path for my rebellion of the *unblessed*. Take the stolen treasury *money* and persuade them to join your rebellion against Taliba who would never be seen as *funny*. And make sure the merchant and the disciple die so you can later *pretend* to join Taliba's army as a true *friend*. Affanu's wife already wrote a letter to *me*. Asking my help to seek justice for her husband who died by your *decree*. Very soon all will go *away* so I can revive my prophecy without *delay*."

The rebels and I went to Basrah to seek justice and *grace*. Until Taliba confronted us with an army of twenty thousand men as he wished to speak directly to our *face*. He agreed that the rebels needed to be punished for their *disgrace*, but he had to establish order *first*. Upon hearing this Aisha could no longer hide her ruling *thirst*. And so a battle commenced rather *quickly*, in which I killed Talhah by shooting an arrow in the back of his leg rather *swiftly*.

I apologised and said that it was an accident caused by *stress*. After the battle was finished Aisha was escorted away by her younger brother as she felt lesser than *less*.

Al-Marwani I Marwan Ibn Al-Hakam

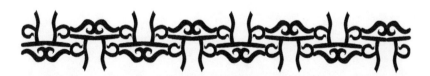

124

125

Muhammad Ibn Siddiqi I Ibn-Shi'ah

"Those who call themselves Muhakkima chose to leave us *behind*. After Muawiyah proved himself to be of an Iblisian *kind*. He cut up the very first Quran in book *form*, showing that his loyalty to Affanu was merely a falsified justice *storm*. So I, Taliba choose you to be the new and improved governor of Egypt's *land*, for you truly are a general who always upholds a just *command*. And if you may ever find yourself in a situation of *danger*, make sure you seek the aid of Malik Al-Ashtar who is anything but a *stranger*."

Before I could even ask Malik for any help he was already killed by Muawiyah and his *crew*. For refusing to denounce Taliba as the true leader in his point of *view*. Muawiyah ordered Malik's killing along with six others while his loyalists simply denied it to be *true*. I managed to govern Egypt for a year until **Al-Kadhaab, The Liar** launched his *coup*.

I was captured without *wait* and when I showed too much verbal resistence they chose to kill me in a manner of *hate*. I was to be stuck inside an already dead donkey's rotten *skin*. And burned alive as they celebrated this unholy *win*. But in the end Allah will punish them for this *sin*.

Ibn-Shi'ah I Muhammad Ibn Siddiqi

Abd Allah Ibn-Abbas I Al-Bahr

"At first I advised my cousin Ibn-Abbas to lead the arbitra-
tion from our *side*. Since he was the only one scholared
enough to destroy Amr's lying *pride*. But you refused so
then I requested Malik Al-Ashtar for the *arbitration*. And
yet again you refused to join my side of the *station*. Since
you wish to elect Abu-Musa then your wish will most cer-
tainly come *true*. But do not cry to me if the results make
people feel *blue*. I did everything I could for the lot of *you*,
but you were simply meant to serve as a disobeying *crew*."

Taliba was actually about to overpower Muawiyah's *forces*,
until he ripped up the first book of the Quran and tied the
pages to the lances of those who rode *horses*. Out of *panic*
the rebels reacted in a manner that would deem them
to be *manic*. They made Taliba retreat his soldiers so the
situation could be handled with *words*. But upon hearing
that an official arbitration was declared they separated
themselves from his army as if they were freed *birds*.

La Hukma Illa Lillah, Judgement Belongs To Allah Alone
a term which was misunderstood in their *head*. I convinced
some of them to return but the others wanted to be *dead*.

Al-Bahr I Abd Allah Ibn-Abbas

127

Qatam Bint Shajna I Bint-Khawarij

"The vast majority of them took heed of my *warning* but the rest preferred to die leaving their loved ones stuck in *mourning*. There were 2.800 of them willing to *battle* and my army of 80.000 men slaughtered almost every one of them as if they were *cattle*. Nine of them survived and managed to escape from our *hand*. Giving them the chance to rebuild for another *command*. No matter what we do they will always exist in the male *seed*, so a woman must always be weary of how to construct a child's *creed*."

When you were selected as a **Successor** my father and brother were happier than any *envoy*. Both of them wished you well as you changed homes from Medina to Kufa as traditions were always yours to *destroy*. Everyone hated the idea of a **Caliph** no longer living in Medina but you never let that spoil your *joy*. But then the call for arbitration proved that you were nothing but a mere Iblisian *toy*.

When I heard that you slayed my family I waited until I met with a survivor, Ibn-Muljam was his *name*. A Jewish convert who directly fell in love after seeing my face of beauty & *fame*. I promised to marry him if he ended your *claim*.

Bint-Khawarij I Qatam Bint Shajna

The Virtues Of Taliba
659 - 661 J

Husayn Ibn Taliba I Al-Husayni

"Why do you keep bringing these crazy men in front of *me*? Surely you do not believe that I would slice one for all of the court to *see*? Verily I care not that any man promised Allah that he would end my *life*. For he has not attempted to do so therefore I could never widow his *wife*. If you hear them curse me then you should simply do the *same*. How else could you possibly uphold the integrity of my *name*? Leave them be for Allah will surely be the one and only to make these evils feel the truest sentiments of *shame*."

Father I must truly say that your poise is way beyond *vision*. After surviving three civil wars you still possess **Sabr, Patience** with absolute *precision*. You were the very first successor to be called a **Mushrik, Disbeliever** in the English *word*. While you merely tried to create a situation in which the killing of your own brethren was *unpreferred*.

But fear not father for Allah will reward you dearly for all of the goodness you have *shown*. Even if those who broke away from your army wanted your death set in *stone*. You will always be the first one to hold the Shi'ah *throne*. Even if Muawiyah's unjust rebellion forces you to stand *alone*.

Al-Husayni I Husayn Ibn Taliba

Husayn Ibn Asadullah
625 - 680 J

129

Hasan Ibn Taliba I Al-Hasani

"Taliba have zero fear for the truth will never come to *light*, since Hasan only tried to uphold his mother's *plight*. I did my very best to make sure poverty and injustice was no *more*. But in my heart I always knew someone would settle the *score*. Make sure to tell Luqman that he is also forgiven for killing *me*. For I was unjust in the sense that Persian difficulties were never mine to *see*. And if you are given a seat at my son Ubaidullah's *trial*. Don't go easy on him for he committed a hate crime so unspeakably *vile*."

Khattabo ever since I saw you harm my mother I wished you a painful *death*. But upon realising the difficulties of your situation I feel remorse for causing your final *breath*. Since the weight of the world was now placed on my two *shoulders*. But I will follow your lead and make sure to push away poverty & injustice as if they were *boulders*.

Ibn-Muljam attacked my father in the mosque of Kufa at *dawn*. Striking him with a poison coated blade like a true Iblisian *spawn*. My father was praying at the *time*, so he had no clue at all of the upcoming *crime*. The poison killed him two days *later* while I executed Ibn-Muljam the *hater*.

Al-Hasani I Hasan Ibn Taliba

Sajah Bint Al-Harith I Al-Tamima

"My dear oracle, it seems as though it was only *yesterday*. That I saved you from a life of slavery and *decay*. After Musaylimah was killed in the battle where Muslims caused *disarray*. Now here we are eight months after Taliba was *killed*. His son doing a surprising job of preventing further blood from being *spilled*. But I convinced him to abdicate his rule to *me*. After we agreed on a long-standing peace *treaty*. I stated that when I *die* my son will not be nominated as successor but he has no idea that it was all a *lie*."

When I had originally declared to be a prophetess I was a Christian *queen*. So when Tulayha's forces were defeated an alliance with Musaylimah seemed very *keen*. I married him and became his Khadija until he *died*, then Muawiyah rose up to save my *hide*. He brought me to him and informed me that he was Hind's *son*. Right then and there I realised that he was my lucky *one*. So I openly converted in front of *everyone*, for he was the king I saw sitting on a *throne*. Hopefully I could make it come true all on my *own*.

Throughout all of the Caliphates I had been envisioning a way to make my prophecy come true by setting it in *stone*.

Al-Tamima I Sajah Bint Al-Harith

130

Bínt Daughter Of

Siddiqi who set the norm of a just *rule*. Further enriched by Khattabo's *fuel*. If only Affanu was righteous enough to continue the legacy of that *school*. It would've never lead to the civil wars so *cruel*.

Muhammad did say the first Caliphate would never surpass 30 *years*. Aisha heard this sad prophecy while covering her *tears*.

Ãisha

Nicknamed As-Siddiqa as she was a woman proud to state what was *true*. Fighting Affanu's Abd-Shams idea of making leading women go *adieu*.

If only she would've taken heed of the messenger's final *vision*. She would've never paved the way for Muawiyah's *collision*. In the end she really did regret making that *decision*.

131

Aisha Bint Siddiqi I Al-Shemia

"Aisha I know you merely think of me as a younger half *brother*. But I have always respected your values over that of *another*. Until you spun yourself completely out of *control*, launching a rebellion at Basrah that could have meant your execution in accordance with our *scroll*. Even though we came from the same *blood*, I fought on Taliba's side for he was merely making sure the tensions would no longer *flood*. I remember when he wed my widowed mother without *wait*, and hugged me as a son chosen by *fate*."

I was your older *sister* who came from the same *mister*. How I wailed after I heard the words you had for *me*. For a reflection of my recent behaviour caused me anything but *glee*. Thankfully I managed to swallow my *pride*, and apologise to Taliba for my mistakes impossible to *hide*. He accepted my apology and as you returned to his *side*. I saw how you had grown to be a man with the greatest *stride*.

And when I heard about Egypt's *coup* I realised Muawiyah was a true spawn of the evil we all *knew*. You, Malik and the others were tortured to become part of the *dead*. My late husband even had a vision about it once in his *head*.

Al-Shemia I Aisha Bint Siddiqi

Na'ila Bint Al-Furafisa I Al-Uthmaniya

"O Ümmah as I receive this crowning ceremony in Jerusalem, the city of *grace*. I remember that not too long ago Khattabo gave the Jews a right to return after ages of exile and *disgrace*. And now it is up to me to fill the shoes of the **Rashidun** *Caliphate*. **The Rightly Guided Succession** of 4 leaders who governed through endless streams of *hate*. Among them my cousin Affanu who was the *first* to represent the Abd-Shams *thirst*. But he never assigned an *heir* therefore I am the first true Caliph of this house so *rare*."

How I regret the very day that I asked this snake of a man for *aid*. For his perverted dreams of ruling made him set up this entire *crusade*. He was planning to overthrow my late husband from the *jump*. Oh how I feel as though I've been played as a mere *chump*. Muawiyah already sent me multiple letters in which he asked for my widowed *hand*. But I prefer to die than marry into this sinful *command*.

So I sent him three of my teeth in a *bag*, making sure his eagerness to wed me suffered from a *sag*. How it must have killed Muawiyah *inside* to know that my once stunning beauty came undone to avoid being his stupid *bride*.

Al-Uthmaniya I Na'ila Bint Al-Furafisa

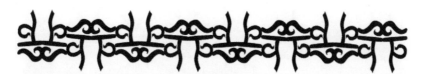

132

Amr Ibn Al-'As I Al-Kadhaab

"I, Abu-Musa wish to undo this lying man's opinion as a pure *disgrace*. For we had both sworn in the name of Allah to stand in front of you all and choose a successor with a different *face*. But this sneaky individual let me speak *first* so he can prove to still be liar who never did away with his power hungry *thirst*. This arbitration was supposed to prove the rebels *wrong*, but he managed to give their barbaric plight a valid reason to *belong*. Maybe our religion truly has been under control of the hypocrites all *along*."

The entire sandy domain of Egypt was conquered by my *hand*. So when Affanu made the decision to relieve me from my *command*, I went mad beyond reason as I risked to lose my legacy so *grand*. So then Muawiyah requested me to join his *side*, I did while constructing the perfect plot to make sure Affanu *died*. Then I was assigned to be myself at the *arbitration*, I tried to bribe Abu-Musa over and over again but he refused to join my side of the *station*.

I had to tell another *lie* even if it made me a bad *guy*. But now I regret all of my past deeds so *sick*, as Fatima's hand keeps showing in my dreams as if it were a vengeful *trick*.

Al-Kadhaab I Amr Ibn Al-'As

Muhammad Ibn-Maslamah I Al-Khazraji

"O Muslims the only thing I can say to *you*, is that Siddiqi
and Khattabo's examples are no longer able to be *true*.
For the first Fitna has schismed us *all*, so my behaviour is
needed if our empire is to avoid a destructive *fall*. There-
fore be glad with what I give you even if you receive little to
none. For the only way my rule can truly succeed is if the
noblemen are granted their superior *fun*. If you disregard
this advice you will surely suffer from *stress*, so make sure
you are happy enough to receive Allah's undying *bless*."

When Muawiyah was building the naval *corps* he often
sailed through India's spicy *door*. His policies were often
influenced by their caste system based on a *lie*. In which
you are to remain what you were born into without a single
chance of soaring through the *sky*. All so he and his noble-
men could never stop playing the role of a ruling rich *guy*.

How on earth did we ever get this *far*? Verily the people
have become blinded by the evils of a shooting *star*. And
when I heard that Basrah's camel battle happened without
wait, I packed up my things and walked past Medina's *gate*.
To spend my last days in a desert tent in solitude of *hate*.

Al-Khazraji I Muhammad Ibn-Maslamah

The Messenger's Knight
591 - 666 J

Hasan Ibn Taliba I Al-Hasani

"Even though Muljam, one of the rebels chose to assassinate me so I can be confronted with Allah's *fate*. Make sure you never forget that they will forever remain your brethren in both love and *hate*. Therefore do not wage war with them to simply try and settle the *score*. For that is a battle that would never stop reaching an *encore*. Make sure that you always follow Muhammad's *path* and fight the evil within yourself to never succumb to *wrath*. For all Muslims should truly aim to prevent another *bloodbath*."

Muawiyah expected me to join him in his expeditions against the rebel *alliance*. But I refused on the basis of not killing my brethren who had chosen *defiance*. Just because I drafted a peace treaty with him does not mean I have to respond to every request with *compliance*. For I know deep within my *soul*, that Muawiyah was the one who fueled the original rebel fire with slandering *coal*. As the mosques that firmly support his *rule*, have introduced daily sessions of cursing out my late father as a weak *fool*.

But in the end he will surely reget every single *decision*, as Allah's retribution hits everyone with absolute *precision*.

Al-Hasani I Hasan Ibn Taliba

Hasan Ibn Asadullah
624 - 670 J

Marwan Ibn Al-Hakam I Al-Marwani

"There is no possible chance for me to outlive Hasan with fair *play*, but luckily Ja'da one of his wives will soon poison him after she agreed to my *sway*. I told her she would get 100.000 dinars plus a marriage with Yazid who I wish to nominate for the *crown*. When she does the deed I want you to bring her to me so she can look at me with a *frown*. For anyone who agrees to my *schemes* deserves a shattering of their *dreams*. As the only one who could outplay me has yet to burst through the unimadjïnnable *seams*."

Ja'da poisened Hasan and joined me to Damascus to collect her *prize*. But Muawiyah changed his mind and instead married her to another man who was large of *size*. After the wedding ceremony her husband took the sum of money from her *hands* and decided to invest it into his *lands*. While she was simply forced to stay in the house as she never stopped regretting her previous *commands*.

When they tried to bury Hasan next to his grandfather according to his *will*. I refused simply because Hasan stated it was unnecessary if it caused the tensions to *spill*. Then Aisha agreed as *well* and Ibn-Abbas wished us all to *hell*.

Al-Marwani I Marwan Ibn Al-Hakam

Marwan I Al-Hakam
626 - 685 J

The Siege Of Constantinople
674-678 J

Yazid Ibn Muawiyah I Ibn-Sufyani

"From the very moment I succeeded rule and launched the Umayad *caliphate*. I set out for a series of brutal campaigns of warfare and *hate*. Particularly against the Byzantine Romans who possessed a territory that I wished to conquer in the name of Allah's *fate*. And now we have a chance to take their capital Constantinople by the *sea*. So I oversaw the construction of a fleat of the largest *degree*. Now I Muawiyah order you Yazid to lay siege on this capital of strategic importance in name of our house's *decree*."

It was a bitter journey that ended in a failure to *win*, as the Byzantine Romans built fortresses to keep their city free of the Umayad *kin*. For years my father continued this campaign by spending buckets of *cash*. While I as the naval commander simply couldn't get their capital to *crash*. Especially when they used magical greek *fire*, to banish our fleat from their protected waters with results so *dire*.

To make things even *worse*, on our way back to Syria we found ourselves stuck inside a devastating storm like a *curse*. After that our reputation truly suffered from a *crack*, as our best efforts were not enough to pick up the *slack*.

Ibn-Sufyani I Yazid Ibn Muawiyah

Yazid Ibn-Sufyani
647 - 683 J

137

Husayn Ibn Taliba I Al-Husayni

"Husayn, my younger brother who I love with all my *heart*, I can only tell you that the one who poisoned me mastered the deceptive *art*. I fear to give you a name that would force you to settle the *score*. And if I ended up being wrong it would mean that your integrity is no *more*. So listen very carefully to the final words I'll say to *you*. Make sure to never go against the treaty unless Yazid is nominated by Muawiyah the *shrew*. For the Kufa loyalists will always try to *lure* your identity into their power struggle for *sure*."

When I accompanied Yazid on his quest to conquer the Byzantine capital in *style*. We ended up developing a bond that consisted of a genuine *smile*. He had become my *friend*, but the reality of our situation was never seen as *pretend*. If he were to go against the islamic *form*. I would be forced to rebel against his house and its ruling *norm*.

The last two years of Muawiyah's *life* I could see that old age was catching up to him as his son prepared for every possible *strife*. And one day my curiosity got the better of *me*, so I followed Yazid to a mosque that was never mine to *see*. I saw Yazid stand up and curse my father's *decree*.

Al-Husayni I Husayn Ibn Taliba

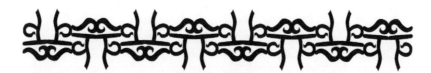

Abd Allah Ibn-Ibadh I Al-Tamimi 2.0

"One day Muhammad summoned for me while I was eating my *meal*. So I snubbed him and finished off my plate making my food unable to *steal*. Muhammad then cursed me and wished my belly would never *fill*, now in my final days I realise what that meant as I find myself preparing for Allah's *kill*. I was to succumb to the basic principles of merciless *greed*, that is why I did so much evil to forcefully take the crown while abusing the divine *creed*. Allah I beg of you please forgive me for the evils I had done *indeed*."

I was a young commander at Nahrawan's *battle*, firmly standing behind my leader Al-Rasibi until Taliba's forces slaughtered us as if we were *cattle*. I along with eight other men managed to *flee*, for I had tasted war for the very first time and it set me *free*. Of all idolatrous notions as I now stood firmly in my belief of Muhammad's *decree*.

Muawiyah had lied to my commander and told him that he would *attack* Taliba directly in the *back*. But it was all a lie told by this bad *guy* and when I escaped he gave me a *goal*, As Yazid's servant spying on everyone's *soul*. When the evil Muawiyah died I saw a chance to turn his legacy to *coal*.

Al-Tamimi 2.0 I Abd Allah Ibn-Ibadh

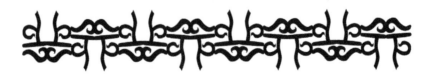

140

Abd Allah Ibn-Abbas I Al-Bahr

"I know you want me to launch a rebellion here in Mecca's safe *space*, but the Kufa loyalists have been sending me constant letters promising to support my claim in this title *race*. Yazid's nomination goes against the very principle of Siddiqi and Khattabo's *school*. So therefore I will always rebel against his claim even if it makes me look like a useless *tool*. For I would rather die as a martyr than continue on living like a *fool*. There's a chance you may disagree with what I think is *right*. For I always believe it's better to stand against an oppressor in both discussion and *fight*."

I myself always preferred peace over *war*, for I never had the opportunity to allow the warrior within me to *soar*. 60 years of absolute tyranny is always better than a rebellion even if it lasted but one *day*. For this second **Fitna** is merely a continuation of the first **Great Divide** that never went *away*. It was merely silenced by a treaty that would never *last*, as the tensions between both sides would always cause a *blast*. If only we could return to our glorious *past*.

For now the only thing I can *do* is focus on the battle of ignorance where hatred will be what people choose to *spew*.

Al-Bahr I Abd Allah Ibn-Abbas

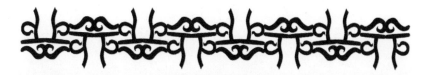

"The greatest Jihad is to battle your own soul, to fight the evil within yourself."
Muhammad

Muhakkima | The Unjudged

"Be in this life as if you were a
stranger or a traveler on a path."
Muhammad

"Let me alone, and go in search
of someone else."
Ali - Taliba

الخوارج

Al-Khawarij | The Exiteers

Al-Azariqa | The Blues

"Let not your love become attachment
nor your hate become destruction."
Umar - Khattabo

"The best among you is the one who doesn't harm others with their tongue or hands."
Muhammad

Al-Abadiyah | The Muslims

Ìbn Son Of

Abbas, Muhammad's uncle often regarded as big-*boned*. Before the battle of Badr his conversion was often seen as *postponed*. And yet there was never a time when the messenger felt close to *disowned*.

As the Hashims usually tend to have each others *backs*. Especially with the Quraish instigating the people's hateful *attacks*.

Äbbas

Born three years before
the Hijra took *place*. When
Banu Hashim was still ex-
iled as Mecca's *disgrace*.
A youthful scholar who
studied the Quran directly
from the prophet's *face*.

After the Rashidun reign
he became fully *grown*.
With a vast sea of knowl-
edge that he discovered
on his *own*. The Professor
who chose to stand *alone*.

Abd Allah Ibn-Abbas I Al-Habib 2.0

Husayn I warned you more than once not to *go*, for Ubaidullah the governor was an evil you could never possibly *outgrow*. You sent your nephew Muslim Ibn-Aqeel to march for Kufa, Iraq and preach support in your *name*. But Ubaidullah interrupted and killed him without a single chance of exiling him in *shame*. He wasn't even allowed to inform you of his clearly unsuccessful *attempt*. Leaving you with a great deal of uncertainty in the form of mental *torment*. So you gathered together 110 of your strongest *forces* and marched for Kufa after mounting your *horses*.

During the long journey you were intercepted by Yazid's men headed by Ubaidullah who carried a face of evil *indeed*. 5.000 men that slaughtered your crew in a manner that went against the messenger's *creed*. As they mercilessly beheaded you and your six month old *son*. But fear not for Allah will surely condemn every participating *one*.

"Shi'ahs I urge you not to rebel for it is not okay to do *so*. For the spilling of Muslim blood is not at all permissible to Allah whom we all are supposed to *know*. Do not repeat the same evils that were performed by your damned *foe*."

Al-Habib 2.0 I Abd Allah Ibn-Abbas

141

The Heroine Of Karbala
680 - 681 J

142

Abd Allah Ibn-Abbas I Al-Habib 2.0

Al-Husayni's son Ali was the only one who did not partake in the *battle* in which all of the messenger's kin were slaughtered as if they were *cattle*. For he had fallen rather *ill* making it unable for him to wield a blade no matter the power of his *will*. When the battle was over Yazid's soldiers wanted to end him as *well*, but his aunt Zainab jumped on his body and protected him by cursing the soldiers to *hell*.

They backed away very fast and took them *all* to Yazid's court in Damascus, Syria to witness the aftermath of their bloody *fall*. Along with Ali, 200 women and girls were taken prisoner without *wait* but Zainab never stopped barking at Yazid even if he would make her suffer a gruesome *fate*. When he ordered her to unveil herself she marched forth and did exactly *so*. Then she gave a stern sermon in which she used a verse of the Quran many have yet to *know*.

... Quran Sura 03: Al-Imran / The Family Of Imran
03. Let not the unbelievers think that our respite to them is good for themselves. For we are only giving them the time to increase their sinning *ways*. For them there will be a punishment far beyond humiliation forever and *always*.

Al-Habib 2.0 I Abd Allah Ibn-Abbas

Ibn-Abbas I Al-Habr
619 - 687 J

Abd Allah Ibn-Abbas I Al-Habib 2.0

Abd Allah Ibn Al-Zubayr chose to remain in Mecca for he too was against Husayn's *plan*. To march for Kufa, Iraq and launch a rebellion against Yazid the unjust ruling *man*. Upon hearing of the events at Karbala the disciple's son went mad beyond *reason*. Marching through the streets of Mecca to declare the Umayad dynasty of absolute *treason*.

I refused to join him and fled Mecca's vengeful *scene*, to then settle in Ta'If so I can forever remain *unseen*, may Allah guide all of our souls away from a path of the *mean*.

"I give not my bayah to the disciple's *son*, for his father Zubayr was killed as a mere unlucky *one*. He was the easiest prey after abandoning the rebellion while Aisha was ready for war and *decay*. His own son even admitted that his father was scared *straight*. So he left the scene seeking to retreat from his rebellion of *hate*. Upon his exit from Basrah he met a man Amr Ibn-Jurmuz was his *name*. They had a short conversation and agreed to pray next to each other as brothers one and the *same*. When Zubayr bowed in prostration of Allah the *divine*. Ibn-Jurmuz drove a blade through the back of his neck in one swift *line*."

Al-Habib 2.0 I Abd Allah Ibn-Abbas

Abd Allah Ibn-Abbas I Al-Habib 2.0

Yazid suffered from a serious *cramp* while he mounted his horse to leave his *camp*. Apparently it felt as though his intestines were turning upside *down*, until he fell ill on his bed to assign to his son the rights to the *crown*. I had never pledged to Yazid's *madness*, for his father Muawiyah only trained him to be a general who commands warfare and *sadness*. So when he died I felt a sense of *gladness*.

How the **Jahiliya, Ignorance** has taken over all of our *kind*, by bending every single aspect of the truth to make sure certain people's interests are *aligned*. It was time to rise up and spread my *creed*, in which you will most certainly be judged by Allah the divine for each and every *deed*.

"To the ignorant people of this islamic *belief*, if you are fed up with the lies make sure you come to me for some truthful *relief*. For I am the one and only who can help you *grow*, by sharing with you the teachings that I have come to *know*. There shall be no limit even if I am visited by a hundred men at the same *time*. For turning away a believer who seeks to obtain knowledge is the truest of all sinful *crime*. Come to me for I am anything but a useless *mime*."

Al-Habib 2.0 I Abd Allah Ibn-Abbas

Abd Allah Ibn-Abbas I Al-Habib 2.0

La Hukma Illa Lillah, Judgement Belongs To Allah Alone a statement that brought forth the entire rebellious *madness*. After the movement of **Muhakkima, Unjudged** used this statement to break away from Taliba's army bringing the Shi'ah dream a great deal of *sadness*. Those who left before the arbitration sought to perform a **Kharaja, Exit** in the English *word*. There was not that much I could do for them as they have always wished to be as free as a *bird*.

But the ones that left after the arbitration's result actually listened to what I had to *say*. I was able to bring them back by explaining the history of the Hudaybiyyah treaty's *way*.

"O **Tabi'un, Followers** of the messenger's *creed*, make sure to always think twice before joining **Al-Khawarij, The Exiteers** who wish to make the two-sided thinkers *bleed*. If you join for the right *reason*, then the chance is very unlikely for you to commit *treason*. However if your reasons are *unjust*, then you will surely succumb to the powers of *lust*. Be aware of freedom as a responsibility instead of a *right*. If not then throughout the realms of time will your colliding desires build up towards a destructive *fight*."

Al-Habib 2.0 I Abd Allah Ibn-Abbas

The Secret Pilgrimage
J 684 - 65 H

146

Abd Allah Ibn-Abbas I Al-Habib 2.0

Upon hearing the news that the exiteering division was *made*, the disciple's son invited all of them to Mecca for a secret pilgrimage in which no man was allowed to carry a *blade*. Of course Nafi preferred to neglect this *rule* and preached in the eye of the public as another violent *tool*.

Thankfully two of my most favored students were present as *well*, Ibn-zayd and Ibn-Ibadh, a dynamic duo whose loyalties towards me never *fell*. They spoke to the many different factions and managed to find the ones who were scared of their path to the flames of *hell*. Upon gathering them *all* they went to Ta'if so they could hear my *call*.

"As **Al-Khawarij, The Exiteers** you must have more than one question for *me*. So before you start asking them let us begin by enlightening *thee*. I am not here to brainwash your *mind*, for I myself have always been adamant that blind faith does not work well together with the Muslim of *kind*. Logic and reason should always be the *source* that drives your religious *force*. Try to make decisions based on your judgement *alone*, for you have nothing to fear if Allah is the one & only that you should hold dear to the *throne*."

Al-Habib 2. I Abd Allah Ibn-Abbas

Ibn-Abbas I Al-Habr
619 - 687 J

Abd Allah Ibn-Abbas I Al-Habib 2.0

I remember when Nafi mounted his horse just like Aisha did with a camel in Basrah, Iraq during her rebellion so *unjust*. The look on both of their faces clearly suggested that they were led astray by the many powers of *lust*. How can it be that this rebellious story is repeating itself with-out *wait*. We are in the craziest moment of our second **Fitna** and the third **Great Divide** is already looming behind a future *gate*. Allah I beg of you please have mercy on us all as the Iblisian whispers have truly hijacked our *fate*.

Nafi rode from Kufa, Iraq all the way to Damascus, Syria and approached me in front of Al-Marwani's court of the fourth Umayad *school*. At that moment he had just estab-lished his house of Marwani *rule*. After the Sufyani house was broken down far beyond repair by any possible *fool*. Walking up to me sword in *hand* Nafi demanded if the act of prayer was required according to the Quran's *command*.

"O Nafi if I were to say *no*, would you honestly kill me as if I could ever be a *foe*? As a matter of *fact* yes it is written in several **Suras, Verses** of the eternal Quran's *pact*. So go *away* as I am truly allergic to those who were led *astray*."

Al-Habib 2.0 I Abd Allah Ibn-Abbas

Abd Allah Ibn-Abbas I Al-Habib 2.0

Ibn-Zayd & Ibn-Ibadh how proud I am to *see*, that you have separated yourselves from the highly extremist Azariqa *decree*. Abadiyah, a **Madhab, School Of Thought** named after Ibn-Ibadh the deceiving *one*. After publicly criticising the truly horrific massacres of Nafi, the blue named *son*.

While he took the public *route*, Ibn-Zayd remained in the background and allowed the scholar within him to *sprout*. By further developing the teachings everyone talked *about*.

"Those who follow the Abadiyah *way*, always avoid using this title unless you wish to be killed without any *say*. If you want the chance to live a long *life*, then make sure to call yourself **Al-Muslimeen, The Muslims** whether husband or *wife*. And if they want more call yourself **Ahl-Al-Istiqaama, The People Of Straightforwardness** who lean neither to the left nor *right*. For both sides are unjust in seeking total power both by day and *night*. The main Abadiya *rule* is that it is unnecessary to have one sole leader to manage every single *school*. And if such a unitarian leader is impossible to be *found* then your loyalties must be given to the most righteous and pious candidate of your diverse *ground*."

Al-Habib 2.0 I Abd Allah Ibn-Abbas

148

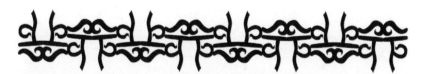

Abd Allah Ibn-Abbas I Al-Habib 2.0

After Yazid died his son Muawiyah II became the third **Caliph, Successor** of the Umayad *realm*. But he was a relatively unknown pushover so the people were very weary of wearing his *helm*. He ruled for no more than four months before he *died*, after that Marwan took over to become the fourth as the qareen of Abu-Sufyan most certainly *cried*.

For this succession marked the end of the Sufyani line, Leaving the Umayad power structure in Marwani hands anything but *divine*. The Marwanid ruling house that brought many a great deal of *fear*. For in the gossipping world he is the one made our brotherly love *disappear*. But that changed when his son usurped the *crown*, by exposing his father in front of the entire court with a *frown*.

"Father, it was you who brought our house so much *shame*, as your slippery demeanor made everyone feel disgusted when hearing our *name*. I vow in front of the entire court that I am Allah's truly chosen *king*. So pledge your loyalties unto me as I make sure my evil father abdicates his throne of *bling*. The history books will never write about how I made your execution pass by as a mere *fling*."

Al-Habib 2.0 I Abd Allah Ibn-Abbas

149

Abd Allah Ibn-Abbas I Al-Habib 2.0

Abd Al-Malik's ascension brought the second **Fitna** to an *end*. By portraying the disciple's son as a man of mere weakness and *pretend*. But the third **Great Divide** is already hiding behind a future *door*, for the classist society of Umayad values will always continue to breed rebellion and *war*. How else would the noblemen's pockets *soar*?

In my last *years* I had set up house in the orchard that Muhammad and Zayd The Beloved fled to after they were bullied away with hatred bringing both of them to *tears*.

"Oh dear **Tabi'un, Followers** of the messenger's *way*, my final days are near so listen up to the last words I have to *say*. I left my door open for council to all of you each and every *day*. Answering your often stupid questions to make sure your sentiments of fate would never *decay*. Please take heed of everything that was *said*, if you don't then I'll make sure to have my scholarly qareen implement nightmares inside your *head*. For that is a curse none of you would like to *feel*, so make sure that Muhammad's message becomes unable to *steal*. For it will only cause further tensions that make sure all of us are unable to *heal*."

Al-Habib 2.0 I Abd Allah Ibn-Abbas

150

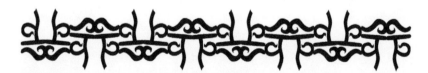

Ìbn Son Of

Zayd, a man who history deemed to be *unknown*. There's no way to tell if he lived to see his son fully *grown*. At the very least he would've been proud to see him ascend the academical *throne*.

An ascension that made him the only real mufti in Basrah at that *time*. Throwing down fatwas to decrease religious *crime*.

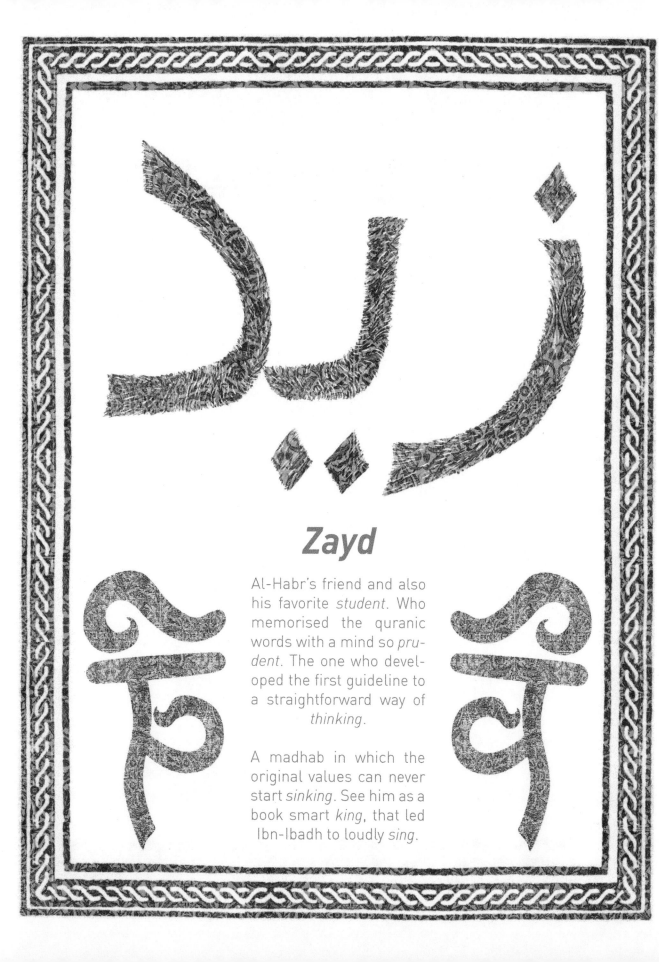

Zayd

Al-Habr's friend and also his favorite *student*. Who memorised the quranic words with a mind so *prudent*. The one who developed the first guideline to a straightforward way of *thinking*.

A madhab in which the original values can never start *sinking*. See him as a book smart *king*, that led Ibn-Ibadh to loudly *sing*.

Jabir Ibn-Zayd I Al-Mukhles 2.0

Muawiyah went on his final pilgrimage and visited every-one who refused allegiance to Yazid including Ibn-Abbas my most favored *teacher*. Threatening every single one of them with force as if he were the truest Iblisian *preacher*.

"Upon hearing about the events of Karbala's *head*. I, Jabir no longer remain in the school of Siddiqi and Khattabo as their legacy is now forever *dead*. I shall join the **Muhak-kima, Unjudged** and build a faction where true devotion is *key*. A faction that goes by the name **Sufriya** for all of the people to *see*. The title of this group is a mere reference to the **Yellowfaced** people that choose to follow *me*. The only true Mufti of Basrah, Iraq who studied our faith from 70 different **Sahabas, Companions** who were all present when Muhammad was building his *decree*. If they could see what the Umayad dynasty has done with our principles they would surely feel rage beyond every possible *degree*. The time has come to step away from the **Su-Shi** *divide*, as both **Sunni** & **Shi'ah** have become obsessed with saving their own *hide*. So therefore let us truly digress from the previous path of those that *lied*. For is it not proof enough that on their deathbed all of them uncontrollably *cried*?"

Al-Mukhles 2.0 I Jabir Ibn Zayd

151

The Heroine Of Karbala
680 - 681 J

Jabir Ibn-Zayd I Al-Mukhles 2.0

The events of Karbala will never be erased from our his-
tory for *sure*. As it shall forever be known as the day that
the **Ümmah, Community** chose to follow an Iblisian *lure*.

By disobeying Siddiqi's main combat *rule*, leaving behind
a rupture of ideals strong enough to brainwash even the
most peaceful *tool*. But luckily Zainab managed to get ev-
eryone's mind back to normal after making Yazid look like
a *fool*. When people heard that she was forced to unveil
her *head*, many women started wearing it as a symbol to
honor her soul even long after she was *dead*. She started
her speech in true scholarly *style*, by giving a stern intro-
duction where no individual would dare again to *smile*.

"In name of Allah the *divine*, the most gracious and merci-
ful whose entire universe serves as a *shrine*. All praise is
due to Allah, the sustainer of the worlds we live *in*. May
praise and salutations also be upon my grandfather Mu-
hammad who most likely died without a single form of
sin. Let us remember that Allah chose Muhammad as
a prophet to bring home a truly pious *win*. So how can it
possibly be that no one condemned the killing of his *kin*?"

Al-Mukhles 2.0 I Jabir Ibn Zayd

152

Ibn-Zayd I Abu-Abadiyah
632 - 712 J

153

Jabir Ibn-Zayd I Al-Mukhles 2.0

Abd Allah Ibn Al-Zubayr how could you use Husayn's death as a mere *tool*. To launch a prophetic rebellion against Ya-zid the greatest Umayad *fool*. Ibn-Ibadh chose to join your *side* because he believed you could undo the *divide*. But I along with Ibn-Abbas know better than to follow such a fake *lure*. For you are not at all your father's son for *sure*.

"People of Basrah, let me tell you a little fact about Zubayr The Disciple of Muhammad the *wise*. He was the only one who never made Muhammad's legacy risk a certain *demise*. For when people were quoting his words in a time of mournful *pain*. He stayed silent because it was the one and only way to preserve the messenger's *name*. For people are too unjust and ungrateful not to abuse his sayings for their very own *claim*. But Zubayr would never bring the messenger's legacy any *shame*. As Muhammad clearly stated to him that those who twist his words have a special place waiting for them in the *fire*. So therefore I re-fuse to follow every single leader of the mainstream *wire*. For the seeds of Iblisian dissention have already been set without *wait*, if you truly want to achieve a level of piety then you must save yourself from a certain hellfire *fate*."

Al-Mukhles 2.0 I Jabir Ibn Zayd

The Fall Of A Mad King
11/11/683 J

Jabir Ibn-Zayd I Al-Mukhles 2.0

Yazid, from the very moment you succeeded Muawiyah's *rule*. You sought to appoint me as a governor in hopes of strengthening your Umayad *school*. For among all of the learned scholars in the islamic *realm*, I was the only one the great professor Ibn-Abbas was unable to *overwhelm*.

He may have been my teacher *first*, but over time it was I who managed to quench his learning *thirst*. And with the unlawful succession my personal opinions regarding the Umayads and their false dynasty are at their very *worst*.

"O Yazid, how could I possibly accept a position of governing based on your ruling *greed*. When everyday I openly preach against those that follow the Umayad *creed*. I shall refuse to join you every single time for I prefer to remain at peace with my soul *indeed*. Everyday I shall march the streets of Basrah, Iraq to preach the messenger's original *way*. Hoping that one day the people would no longer adhere to your greedy *sway*. For there will surely come a *time* where you will be repaid for every single *grime*. You may think to be invincible while you are still *young*, but soon you will find that the pain of truth pierces every *lung*."

Al-Mukhles 2.0 I Jabir Ibn Zayd

154

Ibn-Zayd I Abu-Abadiyah
632 - 712 J

155

Jabir Ibn-Zayd I Al-Mukhles 2.0

Back when the arbitration at Siffin, Syria was *declared*, Ibn-Ibadh along with many others followed Al-Rasibi to perform a **Kharaja, Exit** while remaining *unscared*. They were known as the first wave of **Khawarij, Exiteers** in the English *word*. A group simply wishing to be free as a *bird*.

The **Muhakkima, Unjudged** broke away after hearing the arbitration's *result*, as Allah is the one and only to *consult*.

"O Sufriya let me tell you right now that I am no longer the leader of this *group*. For you have allowed yourselves to become perverted by Nafi, the commander of the barbarian *troop*. I shall always prefer to uphold the standards of **Muhakkima, Unjudged** until the very day I *die*. For those standards are the closest thing we have left to Allah's message now perverted in the Damascus *sky*. Since the Umayad ruling system has become highly skilled in the intrinsic art of the *lie*. I shall always prefer not to take an exiteering *stand*, for there's no better way to become your own enemy than by killing those that reject your *command*. Let us forever remain better than the two mainstream *schools*, before our movement fills itself with violent *fools*."

Al-Mukhles 2.0 I Jabir Ibn Zayd

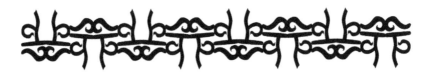

Jabir Ibn-Zayd I Al-Mukhles 2.0

Muawiyah how hard you tried to get everyone to curse Taliba's *name*. Going so far as killing Malik and the others who would rather die than insult the great Asadullah's *claim*. But that strategy backfired as it only made sure that your son Yazid brought the Umayad house great *shame*.

Even the rebels started doing it, making sure Taliba became the most hated figure of *might*. But they were all merely riding the waves of an unjust *plight*. For the messenger clearly praised his brother in faith whose virtues were brighter than every form of *light*. Therefore I *command* all of my men to stop burying their head in the *sand*.

"I know many of you are cursing Taliba's name thinking it belongs to your freedom so *diverse*. But let me inform you that such a notion is Muawiyah's sinful *curse*. Which feeds itself on the already existing cracks by constantly making them *worse*. If you truly believe in Allah's *vision*. Then polity and respect should be the only things that you master with absolute *precision*. Take Nafi's speech at the secret meeting as nothing but a *lie*. For Muhammad was always ready to rise above tribalist tension no matter how *high*."

Al-Mukhles 2.0 I Jabir Ibn Zayd

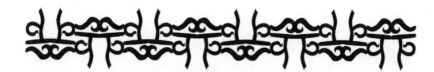

157

Jabir Ibn-Zayd I Al-Mukhles 2.0

I left the **Sufriya, Yellowfaced** as I truly did feel that they were being brainwashed by the radical Nafi founder of Az-ariqa also known as the *blues*. If you dare to disagree with them on any matter they will not even think to make your body *bruise*. But rather grab a sharpened blade and make life or death yours to *choose*. If you repent then they will leave your head *intact*. However if you stand firm in your truth then a beheading will happen in accordance with their *pact*. How vile the likes of man can *be* as the injustices further spread for all of the people to *see*.

I built that faction based on a devotion of the healing powers of *honey*. But excessive greed made them pervert the system while they washed away Nafi's killings with blood *money*. And if one was to question this system they would try to laugh it away with another generic joke anything but *funny*. The ones that did not let it *go* were killed by Qatari Bin Al-Fuja who simply beheaded them as an unholy *foe*.

"No matter how many people label me as the *worst*. I, Jabir will always be known as the *first* to sample a book of holy texts that quenched my professor's learning *thirst*."

Al-Mukhles 2.0 I Jabir Ibn Zayd

Jabir Ibn-Zayd I Al-Mukhles 2.0

Ibn-Ibadh I always saw you as my annoying little *brother* even when you joined the rebels on their destructive path of the *other*. But when you escaped Nahrawan's *battle* where nearly all of the first wave of **Khawarij, Exiteers** were slaughtered as if they were *cattle*. You came back and I saw a true change in your *heart*, as you truly did regret the wrong decisions that you made from the *start*.

"Dear Basrans hear my *cry*, for I choose to stand behind Ibn-Ibadh who seeks to abolish every *lie*. It has been a long time since I saw a leader with such a passion for justice and *reason*. He is without a shadow of a doubt the most pious one even if Nafi seeks his head for *treason*. As all he merely did was critique the Azariqa mindset hellbent on killing every Muslim no matter the *season*. Let us all come together in both body and *mind*, as that is the only way for our sentiments to feel *aligned*. Let us once again *join* the same side of the *coin*. For another twist or *turn* would surely make Muhammad's vigilant heart *burn*. Let us walk the straightforward *path*, where tolerance and kindness outweighs the fundamentals of *wrath*. One more time I would like to *say* that I adhere to Ibn-Ibadh's *way*."

Al-Mukhles 2.0 I Jabir Ibn Zayd

159

Jabir Ibn-Zayd I Al-Mukhles 2.0

"Unlike Ibn-Ibadh I have yet to find a negative *side* of the fifth **Caliph, Successor** of the Umayad dynasty who aim to *divide*. Also the second one of the Marwani house of *rule*. For those of the Abadiyah follow the scholar and not the man who leads the *school*. Differing opinions regarding religious or social judgement should never bring one to *kill*. For in Allah's metaphorical eyes such a deed can never wash away the unholiest blood that was chosen to *spill*.

I would prefer to make good use of my **Sabr, Patience** for change never happens in a *day*. It will prove to be a very long journey for us to no longer feel led *astray*. Let us remain peaceful unlike the Azariqa who declared war on Abd Al-Malik's throne of earthly *clay*. For Ibn-Ibadh has perfectly led us *away* from their violently barbaric *sway*. If you prefer **Tahkim, Arbitration** or **Jihad, Warfare** to someone of the Abadiyah school it makes no difference *anyway*.

We may stand alone in everyone else's *eyes*, but for Allah we are the ones who defined the Quran as a blessing in *disguise*. Taking it too literal only dulls your *imadjinnation* making it unable for you to reach the scholar's *nation*."

Al-Mukhles 2.0 I Jabir Ibn Zayd

Jabir Ibn-Zayd I Al-Mukhles 2.0

"O wonderful professor of mine who was the very first and foremost of his *kind*, you tried to teach us all that Muhammad's original way is what truly heals the *mind*. The Battle Of **Jahiliya, Ignorance** has come to a *halt*. After my alliance with the Umayads had broken down in *fault*. Ibn-Ibadh truly was right from the *start*, as long as there is injustice in our **Ümmah, Community** peace is never what's in our *heart*. It was no wonder that the followers of Abadiyah were growing tired of my scholarly *art*. For I had become a preacher without practicing the teachings for *myself*. No wonder that Ibn-Ibadh's ingenious ideals of the peaceful rebellion made him do so well for *himself*.

I'm simply happy to know that he forgave me for trusting Abd Al-Malik who ordered one of his generals to send us a *spy*. That king is a **Mahdi, Messiah** of Umayads for he can spin a shade of thruthfulness from every single *lie*. If only I could have believed my friend when he warned *me*, but I preferred to wait it out and *see*. In the end both my and Ibn-Ibadh's failures led the terrifying Qatari Bin Al-Fuja to break *free*. From the torturous cell that he was living in after being the sole survivor of Nafi's Azariqa *decree*.

Al-Mukhles 2.0 I Jabir Ibn Zayd

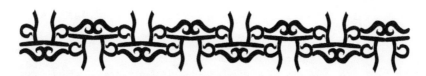

Ìbn Son Of

Ibadh, of the Banu Tamim, one of Arabia's oldest & largest *tribes*. It is often said their ancestor talked about Jesus with one of his young *scribes*. The word Tamim itself relates to their perfect *vibes*.

As they pass through religion just like an arrow passes through an *object*. Reciting the Quran as if they have a vocal *defect*.

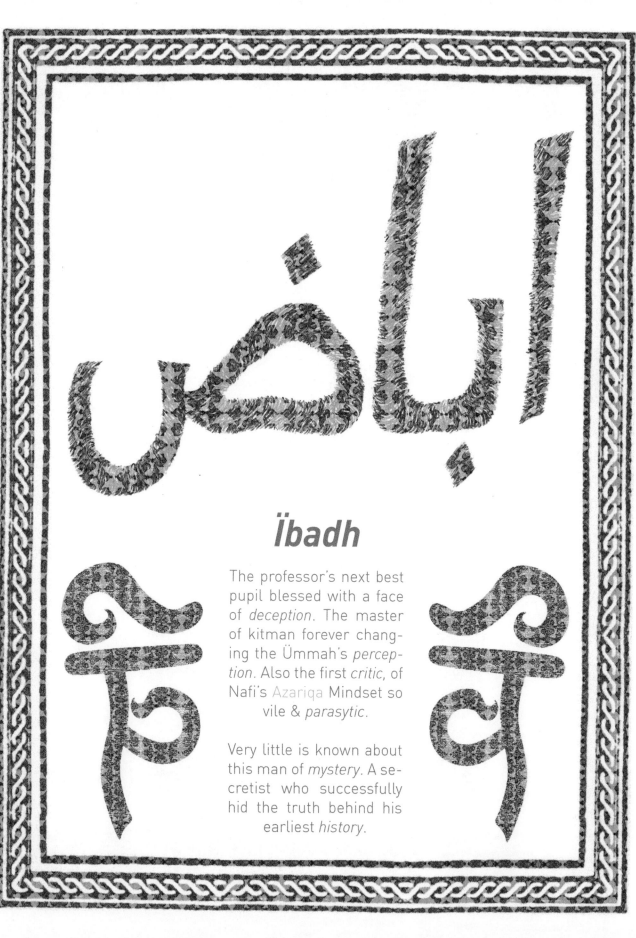

Ïbadh

The professor's next best pupil blessed with a face of *deception*. The master of kitman forever changing the Ümmah's *perception*. Also the first *critic*, of Nafi's Azariqa Mindset so vile & *parasytic*.

Very little is known about this man of *mystery*. A secretist who successfully hid the truth behind his earliest *history*.

Abd Allah Ibn-Ibadh I Al-Tamimi 2.0

After the messenger's male kin was nearly all *dead*, the remaining survivors were counted by the *head*. One young man and 200 women of all different *ages*, upon their public parade to Damascus the Syrian Soldiers were already locking down offers for the unholy sex-slavery *wages*.

In Yazid's court of *bling*, the fallen were presented to the people and the *king*. The heads were left fully unharmed by the governor Ubaidullah may he forever burn in *hell*. For after the ceremony Yazid was given the personal present of Husayn's head in a state not so *swell*. Upon severing his head the soldiers kicked it around as if it were a *ball*. Leaving all of his facial features unable to *recall*. But Yazid knew it was his friend *indeed* as tears started dripping from his chin just like his father Muawiyah had *decreed*.

"Ubaidullah the governor promised he would deal gently with Husayn as he knew him way back *when*. I should've realised it was a lie there and *then*. For Ubaidullah had rejected Muhammad's path at a very young *age*. After his father told him that his succession was already approved by my late father Muawiyah stuck inside a hellfire *cage*."

Al-Tamimi 2.0 I Abd Allah Ibn-Ibadh

The Heroine Of Karbala
680 - 681 J

Abd Allah Ibn-Ibadh I Al-Tamimi 2.0

Dear Zainab you were everything you needed to *be*, a courageous Umm who inspired *me* to break *free*. From servitude to the house of Umaya that went against the **Sunnah, Teachings** of the messenger for everyone to *see*. They adapted the message without a single form of *shame*, as to them it served as a mere strategy to a bigger *game*.

Of ruling a diverse *society* by portraying the fakest form of all *piety*, the calls to prayer have never been more loud and *clear*, but the cultural practices are making our undying faith *disappear*. Zainab your sermon against the evil Yazid brought me *chills*. For you put him down in front of his entire court as everyone did feel your vengeful *thrills*.

"Yazid, you may *employ* your deceit and cunning efforts until it tickles your *joy*. But I swear by Allah that the disgraceful *shame* which you have now earned shall never be erased from the Umayad *name*. Do you think that we have *grown* hopeless after your unjust muscles were *shown*? Or by killing the messenger's male *kin*, you can somehow repent and immediately wash away this *sin*? Take heed of this quranic verse for it shall serve as my scholarly *win*."

Al-Tamimi 2.0 I Abd Allah Ibn-Ibadh

162

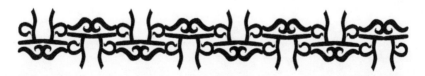

Ibn-Ibadh I Ibn-Abadiyah
644 - 708 J

Abd Allah Ibn-Ibadh I Al-Tamimi 2.0

After Al-Husayni's *death*, the disciple's son rose up in one swift *breath*. He preached non-stop to both meccans and medinans without *wait*. Marching through every street and preaching to every *gate*. The citizens demanded to speak with Yazid after informing him of this upcoming *hate*.

The answers that were given were simply fairytales told through *lies*. But Karbala still made all of us feel *despise*.

"O servants who are tired of Yazid's tyrannical *rule*, join me to Mecca so we can make him seen as a *mere* fool. And if you fear the path of the unjust *one*, never forget that Muawiyah neglected the **Sunnah, Teachings** by appointing Yazid his very own *son*. Khattabo's qareen must already be dead after seeing the events of Karbala's *head*. Yazid's forces already took over Medina in a matter *violence*, so let us aid the disciple's son who chose to no longer uphold the public *silence*. Let us *join* his side of the *coin*, for you have nothing to *fear* if you follow the rules of the Mufti in Basrah, Iraq whose presence is always *here*. As he is my metaphorical brother to which my allegiance will never *disappear*. For Jabir Ibn-Zayd is the one & only just *seer*."

Al-Tamimi 2.0 I Abd Allah Ibn-Ibadh

Abd Allah Ibn-Ibadh I Al-Tamimi 2.0

During the siege of Mecca, Yazid passed away rather *unforeseen*, leaving the Umayad ruling system with fractures of the *obscene*. He called for me to visit him on his final *days*, but I refused to do so after witnessing his tyrannical *ways*. For his soul never stopped being an Iblisian *phase*.

Just before Muawiyah joined the dead after breaking down in *tears*, he saw a sudden glimpse of the near future no more than three *years*. What he saw made him realise that Yazid had *lied* when he accepted his father's last wish after his fake tears had *dried*. That *reflection* made Muawiyah seek repentance with Allah the one and only of *perfection*.

"My son Yazid, when I appoint you as **Caliph, Successor** your opposers will come from two *streams*. The first shall be Husayn who will seek to redeem his late Father Taliba's broken *dreams*. Make sure to deal with him gently as he is part of the messenger's *kin*. For if you brutalise Husayn tears will never stop dripping from your *chin*. The violence should be left for Abd Allah Ibn Al-Zubayr also known as the disciple's *son*, as he carries the threat of a lucky *one*. If you don't end *him* he will take over the rebellious *hymn*."

Al-Tamimi 2.0 I Abd Allah Ibn-Ibadh

164

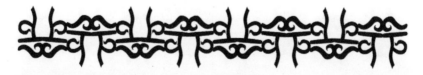

Abd Allah Ibn-Ibadh I Al-Tamimi 2.0

The basic principles of our movement are nearing their *end*, for my former ally Nafi sought to change them with violent *pretend*. They were seeking to commit another **Kharaja, Exit** just like I had *done*. But I realise now that my decision was made from the viewpoint of an unjust *one*. For in matters of justice and *war*, the art of **Tahkim, Arbitration** should be used and promoted in every single *door*.

"O people who have chosen to abandon the **Muhakkima, Unjudged** movement where freedom used to *decree*. I shall never truly join the title of **Khawarij, Exiteers** until all of our understandings reach a similar *degree*. For I am hearing a blues of whispers to name all of the outsiders as **Kafirs, Unbelievers** so we can destroy their *rule*. Our party never used to stand for such actions of a violent millitary *tool*. So therefore I shall never truly accept this newfound title of an exiteering *fool*. But for now I shall remain with *you* along with the Umayad servants who joined my side instead of the *blue*. But once the radicals take *over* our allegiance shall die away like an imadjïnnary *clover*. For I am a **Tabi'i, Follower** of the messenger's *way*, after his cousin Ibn-Abbas made me the scholar I am *today*."

Al-Tamimi 2.0 I Abd Allah Ibn-Ibadh

Abd Allah Ibn-Ibadh I Al-Tamimi 2.0

How happy I was that the leaders of the former **Muhak-kima, Unjudged** movement *agreed*. To go on this secret pilgrimage to meet Abd Allah Ibn Al-Zubayr the shadow leader of Mecca *indeed*. I will offer him a deal that could potentially restore Siddiqi and Khattabo's justice *creed*.

The night before we leave I will pray until the darkest *sky* passes the unseen *eye*, when sunlight outshines every *lie*.

"O son of Zubayr I swear a vow to unite all of the **Khawarij, Exiteers** under *you*. If you agree to establish order based on the pious *two*. Siddiqi and Khattabo's legacy must be the pillars of this rule that many **Tabi'un, Followers** of the faith never *knew*. For Affanu was only just in his first six *years*, and Taliba's reign became unjust when it reached the second half that left him heartbroken with *tears*. If you *agree* I will give my **Bayah** for all to *see*, it shall serve as a **Pledge** to honor the greatness that could be *thee*. I urge you to think it *through*, for you could build a dynasty where all of the people benefit instead of only the superior *few*. The offer only lasts until this pilgrimage's final *day*, let me know if you can accept this totally non-conflicting *way*."

Al-Tamimi 2.0 I Abd Allah Ibn-Ibadh

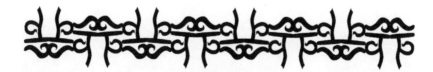

Abd Allah Ibn-Ibadh I Al-Tamimi 2.0

I remember the day Aisha mounted her camel so *clear*. Especially now that Nafi is following in her footsteps no longer *here*. He decided to label everyone that disagreed with a **Khariji, Exiteer** as a **Kafir, Unbeliever** who needs to *die*. Whether male, female or child the killing of such people required not a single *cry*. For the killings are merely what happens when blue takes a firm interest in bloody *red*. Making sure that there is nothing holier than giving someone from **Dar Al-Kufr, House Of Unbelief** a fate of the *dead*. Preferably by severing their screaming *head*.

But luckily I was able to separate my following from his with *success*. As I have truly been enlightened after reading the book of Jabir's *bless*. The Diwan consisting of 1.000 *pages* filled with lectures from the eldest Muslim *sages*.

"O Nafi you *claim* that you do these acts in Allah's eternal *name*. But you are merely a twisted soul bringing his religion a great deal of *shame*. You have created a *curse* that throughout the realms of time will continually grow *worse*. But the people will always remember me as the very first true *critic*, of your Azariqa mindset so vile and *parasytic*."

Al-Tamimi 2.0 I Abd Allah Ibn-Ibadh

Abd Allah Ibn-Ibadh I Al-Tamimi 2.0

When Abd Allah the disciple's son refused to accept my *plea*, I sought to rid myself of all leading influences in an attempt to be *free*. It was time to develop a faction that separated from the **Ümmah, Community** in every *degree*.

"Sunnis, Shi'ahs, Qadaris, Mu'tazilis, Muji'is and all of my former allies from the exiteering *realm*. To all of thee I would like to openly state that I reject to wear your *helm*. For you are all in search of a supposed truth only to make up your own *lie*. For Allah has no body therefore it is sinful to think of the divine as a sugardaddy in the *sky*. Or an invisible force used as a mere tool to silence the *why*.

The throne that is mentioned in the undying quranic *book*, is only a metaphor for the endlessly etherial presence of Allah's *look*. No matter where you are Allah is forever present with *you*, so do not think you can deceive the true message with a mindset of the *blue*. For Allah is beyond all forms of *vision* yet we are constantly being watched over by our lord with absolute *precision*. Never forget that to Allah's metaphorical *eyes* we are all equal so undo yourselves of this vile class society based on Umayad *lies*."

Al-Tamimi 2.0 I Abd Allah Ibn-Ibadh

168

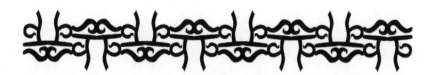

Abd Allah Ibn-Ibadh I Al-Tamimi 2.0

"To those who think that Abd Al-Malik also known as Al-Marwani's *son*. Is pious and just then let me correct you as you have been played as yet another ignorant *one*.

For he is merely wearing a mask that suggests Khattabo's presence to be *near*. But he is still using the same unjust shackles that make sure the class society of Umayads will never *disappear*. For the messenger had clearly stated that the variety of race should be of no issue to us at *all*.

I learned that from **Al-Habr, The Professor** himself when he stated that equality is the only way in which a society will never *fall*. For mutual understanding and peaceful mediation should never be replaced with fake repenting after a truly violent *brawl*. Why on earth would it be so wrong to elect a non-Arab for a successionary *rule*?

For Rouzbeh and his family are some of the most pious of our Abadiya *school*. Especially his young son Rustam who carries an essence similar to that of Taliba The Lion Of Allah the *divine*. As he was born inside a Zoroastrian temple in front of the eternal fire often worshipped as a *shrine*."

Al-Tamimi 2.0 I Abd Allah Ibn-Ibadh

Abd Allah Ibn-Ibadh I Al-Tamimi 2.0

170

" O professor of the Abbas *faction*, let me applaud you for your wonderful strategic action. The **Sunnah, Teachings** of Muhammad have sprouted again as the new seeds will quickly grow into *grass*. I hope you can see it all unfold as Allah determined it was your time to pass. I vow to forever uphold the *tale* of your scholarly spirit without any *fail*.

For besides Muhammad you are the one and only man that all sides choose to *hail*. For your original lessons of *piety*, have given Ibn-Zayd the ability to construct the path towards a perfect *society*. Where the people sin on their own terms but the leader shall always hold on to *sobriety*.

An ancient path where puritanical tolerance and political silence meet each other *halfway*. Serving as a symbolic reference to my talk with him during Nafi's public *disarray*. At a time when you were nearing a fate of the *dead*, we had a discussion about true justice and went toe-to-*head*.

I was so angry after that *talk* that I joined the rioters on their rebellious *walk*. Now I look at that moment of *time*, and pray everyday that I could undo my part in the *crime*."

Al-Tamimi 2.0 I Abd Allah Ibn-Ibadh

Ìbn Son Of

A man named Al-Azraq the Arabic word for *blue*. Whose son Nafi created the first stream of terrifying *glue*. A substance forever to return when hatred is what people *spew*.

Whenever the people are led *astray*. This mindset starts to erupt with the most violent *sway*. Fighting to the very end while never backing *away*.

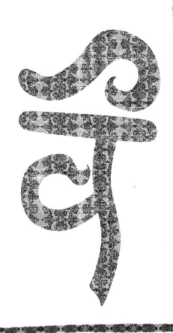

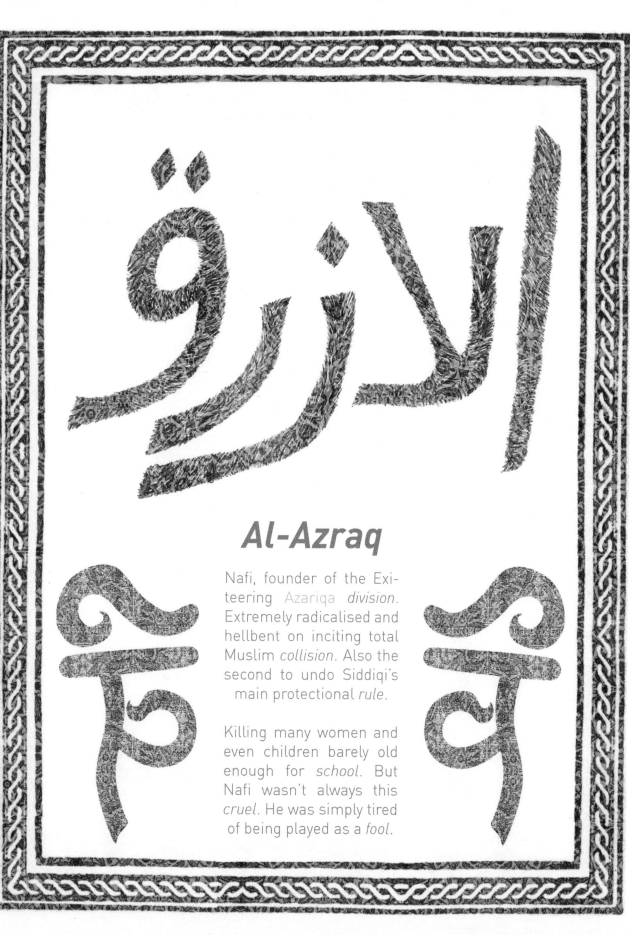

Al-Azraq

Nafi, founder of the Exi-
teering Azariqa *division*.
Extremely radicalised and
hellbent on inciting total
Muslim *collision*. Also the
second to undo Siddiqi's
main protectional *rule*.

Killing many women and
even children barely old
enough for *school*. But
Nafi wasn't always this
cruel. He was simply tired
of being played as a *fool*.

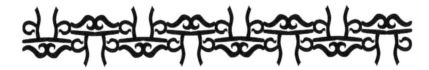

Nafi Ibn Al-Azraq I Al-Munafiq 2.0

Husayn I was your most loyal servant of Kufa constantly sending you letters without *wait*. Hoping that your rebellion against Yazid would result in your army storming our *gate*. But sadly the reputation of your father still brings many of Kufa's residents a great deal of *hate*. Which was only made worse when the governor Ubaidullah made you and your loved ones suffer such a gruesome *fate*.

When Siddiqi's rules of combat were *undone*, the level of **Jahiliya, Ignorance** reached a point of no return as the governor's men had so much *fun*. Husayn and his youngest son Ali who was only six months of *age*. Both had their heads severed and used as a ball much to my *outrage*. After the battle I marched the streets of Kufa where the sense of this tragedy was *strong*. And gave a speech that made sure my side of the story was truthful all *along*.

"O mourning kufans have no *fear*, for the son of blue has risen with a vengeful *tear*. The Muslims are celebrating the death of their messenger's *kin*. So the time has come to slaughter them all for their embracement of *sin*. Kill them whether man, woman or child for that is a true *win*."

Al-Munafiq 2.0 I Nafi Ibn Al-Azraq

Ibn Al-Azraq I Abu-Azariqa
632 - 685 J

The Heroine Of Karbala
680 - 681 J

Nafi Ibn Al-Azraq I Al-Munafiq 2.0

Zainab, not only did you save your nephew from a fate of the *dead*, but you also managed to subdue Yazid's madness in front of his entire court while he forced you to unveil your *head*. You spoke with power so *vast*, even though I only read a report about it I could still feel the truth *blast*.

A 2.0 of Khadija, the Umm of all Muslims no matter the *creed*, as you were the very first one to hold a Majlis *indeed*. A mourning ritual for those of Muhammad's *breed*. I thank you for inspiring my next move as I live and *bleed*.

"My fellow Azraqi's, if a man's honor is under *attack* then a peaceful solution will be found without throwing a single *smack*. But those who dare to harm a woman's *poise* shall receive 80 lashings that make the loudest of all whipping *noise*. For every one of our women shall be seen as a Zainab who was wronged beyond *reason*. After the Umayads used their merciless greed to get the **Ümmah, Community** to commit mass *treason*. But I have found a way to show that we are way better than those *fools*. So from now on stoning a person for merely committing adultery shall be banished from every single one of the exiteering *schools*."

Al-Munafiq 2.0 I Nafi Ibn Al-Azraq

172

Ibn Al-Azraq I Abu-Azariqa
632 - 685 J

Nafi Ibn Al-Azraq I Al-Munafiq 2.0

Abd Allah Ibn Al-Zubayr you were my backup vote for *sure*. So when you started preaching against Yazid I felt compelled to follow your *lure*. But over time I realised that both your souls carried a similar evil impossible to *cure*.

Because of this I chose to break away from your *claim* and sought to create a faction based on my very own *name*. The intolerant mindset shall forever be linked to my brutal *fame*. And when I achieve my quest the Muslims will never again be able to see each other as one and the *same*.

"My fellows of Al-Azariqa, **The Blues** most certainly feared by *all*, for our faction is the only one who holds true to Allah's *call*. Forever and again shall our mindset erupt in this unjust world no matter how many times we *fall*. We will be stopped by none even if we have to climb the highest *wall*. On a serious note the disciple's son will no longer be seen as our *ally*. For even his motives have been corrupted with **Kufr, Unbelief** as everything he told me before turned out to be a *lie*. Do not lose faith in our cause for Allah the divine always graces us with a blue *sky*. Just always remember that every sinning Muslim should *die*."

Al-Munafiq 2.0 I Nafi Ibn Al-Azraq

Nafi Ibn Al-Azraq I Al-Munafiq 2.0

Yazid, the only thing you were truly born for was to serve as an Iblisian *spawn*. For you and your despicable father were both shadows who wished to interrupt the coming of another *dawn*. No one will know the truth about your final moments of *life*. For I gave you a taste of your own medicine as you died by one who was supposed to be your *wife*.

Ja'da who poisoned both her husband and you while the two of you were getting *drunk*. As the situation she was in made her feel quite a hateful *funk*. But she's happy now since I never go back on my word unlike the Umayad *punk*.

"My dearest Ja'da, how glad I am to see you have escaped Damascus safe and *sound*. As you are now in Kufa where Taliba was attacked while prostrating on the *ground*. But fear not for I am not Muawiyah in any way, shape or *form*. So I will make do on my promise to marry you in accordance with the islamic *norm*. The chosen poison for Hasan gave him a relatively painless *death*. But Yazid and the man you were forced to marry truly suffered until their very last *breath*. Which is the correct punishment for a **Kafir, Unbeliever** who deserves to lose *all* as they *fall*."

Al-Munafiq 2.0 I Nafi Ibn Al-Azraq

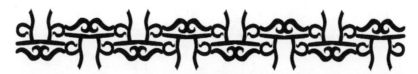

174

Nafi Ibn Al-Azraq I Al-Munafiq 2.0

When Yazid was poisoned by Ja'da my vengeful *wife*, madness and disarray plagued every single aspect of Umayad *life*. It gave the movement of **Muhakkima, Unjudged** the ability to think *free* and come up with our own creed for everyone to *see*. As we were no longer willing to follow the monolith ideas that most people chose to *join*. House Umaya or Hashim, two sides of the same ancestral *coin*.

It was *time* to end the disbelieving *crime*, may Husayn forgive me for portraying his dad as a weak man of *grime*.

"The Azariqa conclusion regarding Taliba's reign will forever be loud and *clear*. He was a disbelieving reformist who sought to uphold the peace in a manner so *queer*. A real leaders fights and kills in Allah's name until the very day he *dies*. Leaving behind a legacy of bloodshed forever to roam around in the *skies*. For Ibn-Ibadh's calls of tolerance and moderation are merely fairytales and *lies*. As he himself is only a puppet of Ibn-Zayd who seeks to change our current ways while forever remaining in *disguise*. If his opinions really are that pious and *good* then he should be the one to spread them around in every racial *hood*."

Al-Munafiq 2.0 I Nafi Ibn Al-Azraq

Nafi Ibn Al-Azraq I Al-Munafiq 2.0

All factions of **Al-Khawarij, The Exiteers** went to Mecca for pilgrimage as a way to solidify our *union*. But little did they know that I had an agenda to conquer the exiteering throne before our second *reunion*. For I was on a *mission* to build a new and improved islamic empire where a beheading would no longer require someone's *permission*.

I would walk to every group of men who seemed angry with the world they *knew*. And inspired them to join my cause with big words that could turn the filthiest water clear *blue*. I would *do* everything to accept killing as *true*.

"From one Azraqi to *another*, let us gather our swords and swear an oath to each *other*. That we would protect and fight for our crew as if we were all sister and *brother*. But never forget that we are the only ones deserving of such *love*. If you do not comply then Allah will surely punish you by closing the gates of paradise up *above*. *Never ever* give in to the highly false sentiments of tolerant *peace*. For our very recent islamic history shows that tribalist tensions will never *cease*. Be who you *are* and fight as if you're a shooting *star*. For every man must have at least one *scar*."

Al-Munafiq 2.0 I Nafi Ibn Al-Azraq

176

Nafi Ibn Al-Azraq I Al-Munafiq 2.0

The time had come to discuss the former **Muhakkima, Unjudged** movement's future *course*. For now we have re-named ourselves **Al-Khawarij, The Exiteers** who chose to break away from the Muslims when I mounted my *horse*.

While all of our factions gathered together I brought my men in front of *me* and presented them with my final *decree*. Spewing true hatred for all of the movement to *see*.

"Oh Azariqa of *mine* show the entire world that you no longer bear a single *shrine*. Declare a violent *war* against other Muslims so the body counts continually *soar*. For they have all proven themselves to be idolatrous monsters in their *heart*. So therefore we should kill them all to make it seem as though the messenger wished it to happen from the very *start*. But beware not to attack the Jews and Christians even if their lifestyle brings you a great deal of *hate*. For they have not yet transgressed against you to shape such a vengeful *fate*. But one day there will come a *time*, when these two groups shall commit against you more than one *crime*. Only then will it truly be allowed by Allah for you to kill them in a manner of bloody *grime*."

Al-Munafiq 2.0 I Nafi Ibn Al-Azraq

177

Nafi Ibn Al-Azraq I Al-Munafiq 2.0

When the Abadiyah school opened its doors to educate every *fool*. I found myself threatened to lose my men to Ibn-Ibadh the puritanically tolerant *tool*. Ibn-Zayd taught him very *well*, but in the end I shall be the one and only exiteering leader exalted from the burning flames of *hell*.

I was going to do whatever it *takes*, to undo their existence before they manage to raise the *stakes*. For they are a looming threat that must disappear by my own *command*, before they actually reach out to shake everyone's *hand*.

"O dear Azariqa brothers of *mine*, if you meet a member of Abadiyah make sure to kill them even if they uphold to Allah's *shrine*. For their ideas are dangerous to our one and only true *goal*. So killing them can be seen as permissible without ever damaging your *soul*. For we are the only ones who carry the truest burden of Allah's *plight*. By brutally killing **Kafirs, Unbelievers** everywhere much to our holy *delight*. So remain on the extreme for every judgement we pass will add conviction to our *might*. Make sure to oppress their views so they can be banished from the public *eyesight*, for we will be the only ones to carry Allah's *light*."

Al-Munafiq 2.0 I Nafi Ibn Al-Azraq

Nafi Ibn Al-Azraq I Al-Munafiq 2.0

Congratulations to you Abd Al-Malik since you are now the new Umayad *king*. The fifth **Caliph, Successor** of the Umayad dynasty after killing the fourth one also known as your father Marwan the slippery *weakling*. Your sudden ascension to the islamic *realm* finally made everyone feel secure enough to wear the current ruling dynasty's *helm*.

But I myself still refused to *bow*, as I openly declared to sever your head in a *vow*. I knew my time was limited from the *start* but I didn't mind since my Azariqa mindset would eventually develop itself into a martyr's truest form of *art*.

"Congrats Abd Al-Malik for you have trapped me with no possible way to escape *death*. So therefore I shall simply order my men to fight your troops until their very last *breath*. For you are no better than your father the *lie*, nor are you any better than Muawiyah who perverted Allah's image to a sugardaddy in the *sky*. Never will the world *be free* from the violent mindset that was originally shaped by *me*. I, who stood firm in his own truth for everyone to *see*. And when the day of return comes my already decayed body will metaphorically fill itself with terrifying *glee*."

Al-Munafiq 2.0 I Nafi Ibn Al-Azraq

180

Qatari Bin Al-Fuja I Al-Azraqi

After Ibn-Ibadh and Ibn-Zayd both made a wrong judge-ment *call*. Qatari Bin Al-Fuja was free to build a new Az-ariqa empire to make the entire **Ümmah, Community** *fall*. Abd Al-Malik's soldiers tortured him far beyond *reason*. While Nafi's widow Ja'da was forced to become a sex-slave to please the Umayad soldiers during every *season*.

So when Qatari was *free* he set forth on a mission to both save and crown Ja'da as the true queen of Azariqa *decree*. Qatari killed all of the men that were in her room seeking unholy *relief*. Upon his rescue she immediately chose to accept his proposed title as both her husband and *chief*.

They managed to rope in a whole bunch of lost *souls* by filling their minds with barbaric killing *goals*. After gather-ing the necessary amount of 40 soldiers with *horses*, they settled in Khoezestan, Persia and built an Azariqa State where Nafi's mindset was what commanded the *forces*.

If you were eager to *join* their side of the *coin*, you had to slaughter a **Kafir, Unbeliever** in front of the court's *eyes*. Within a year Abd Al-Malik brought this state to a *demise*.

Al-Azraqi I Qatari Bin Al-Fuja

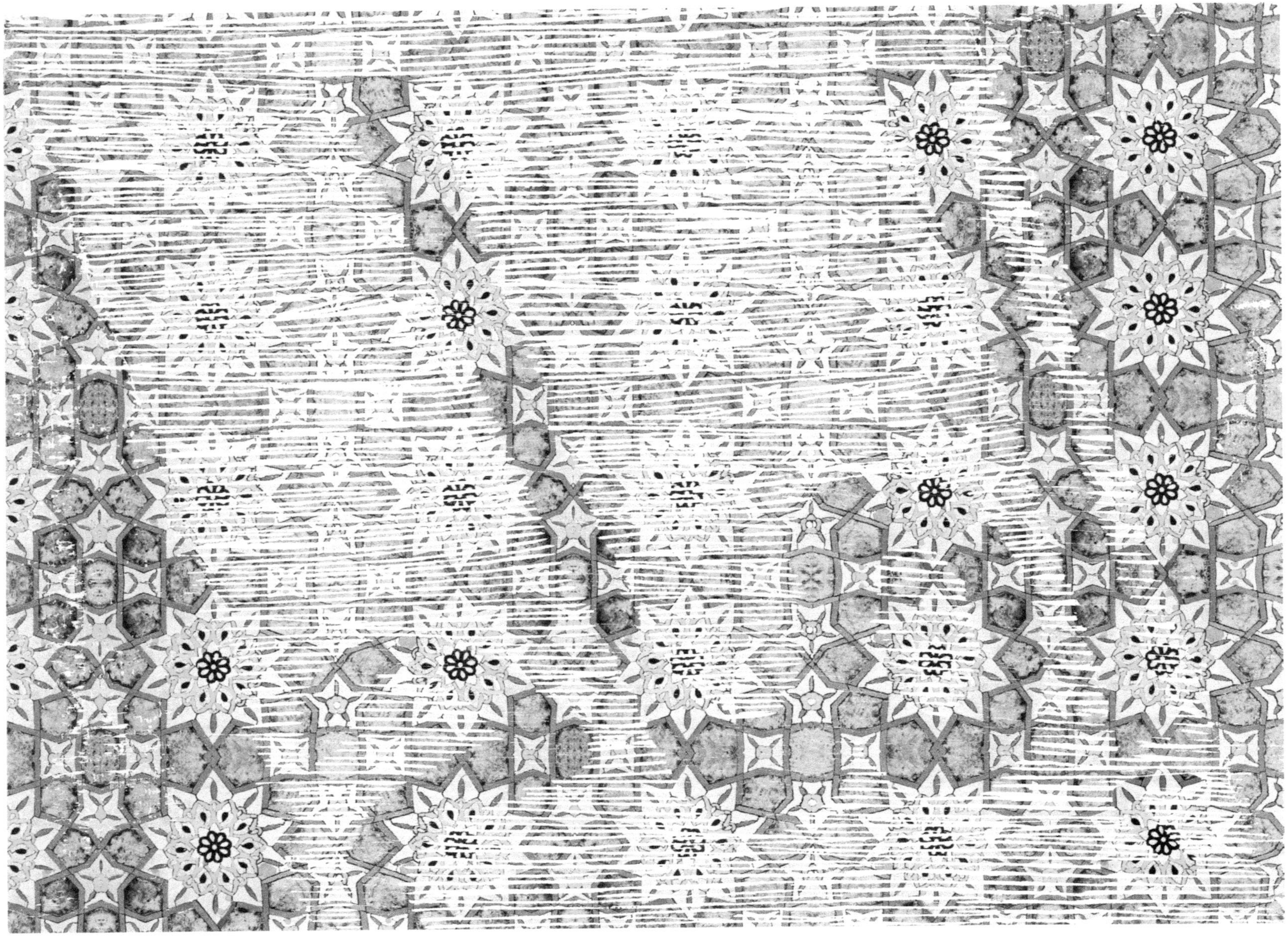

Imam | Islamic Guide

"Don't forget your own self
while preaching to others."
Umar - Khattabo

"I will be patient until even patience
grows tired of my patience."
Ali - Taliba

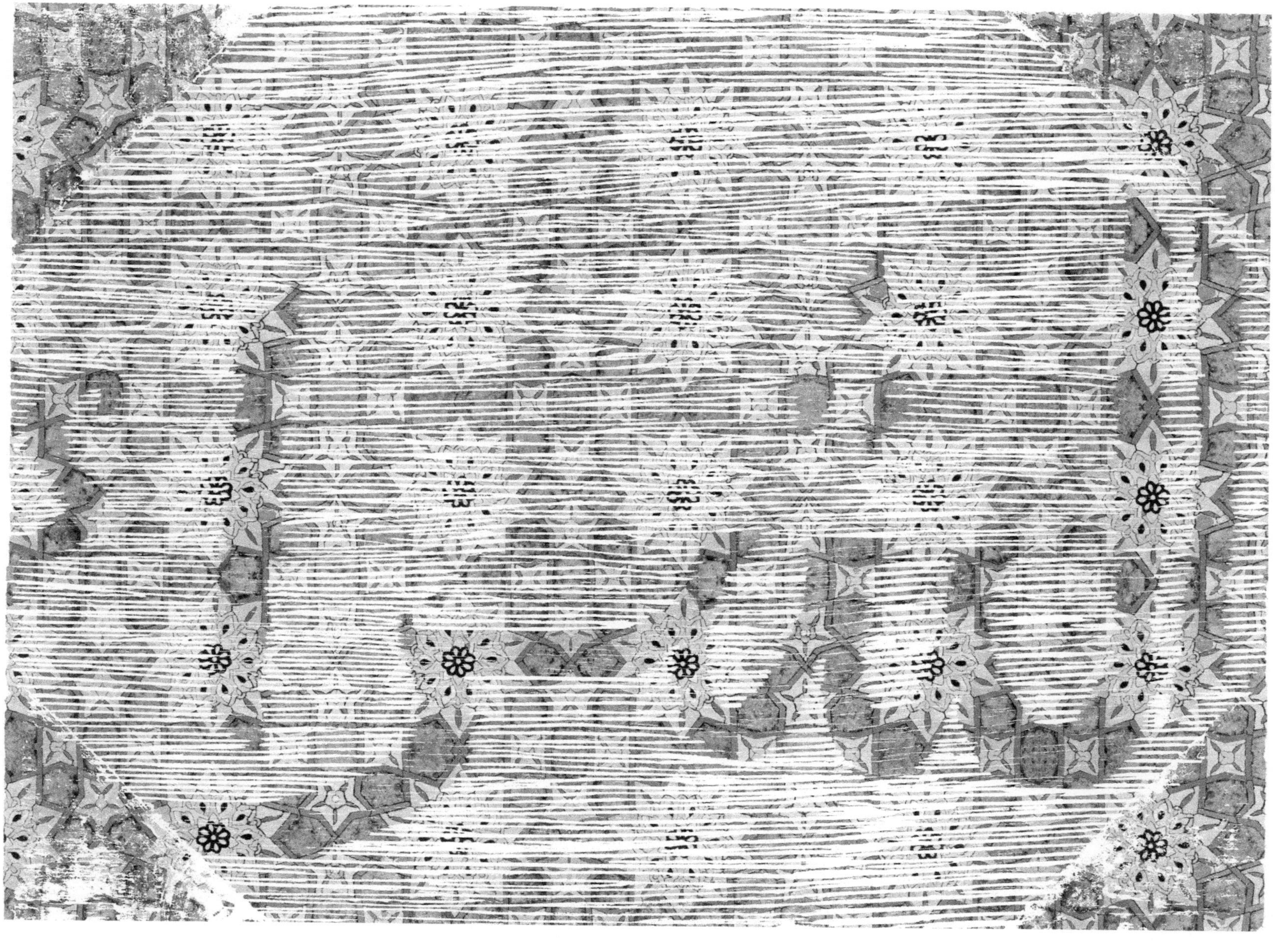

Al-Sha'raa | Activism

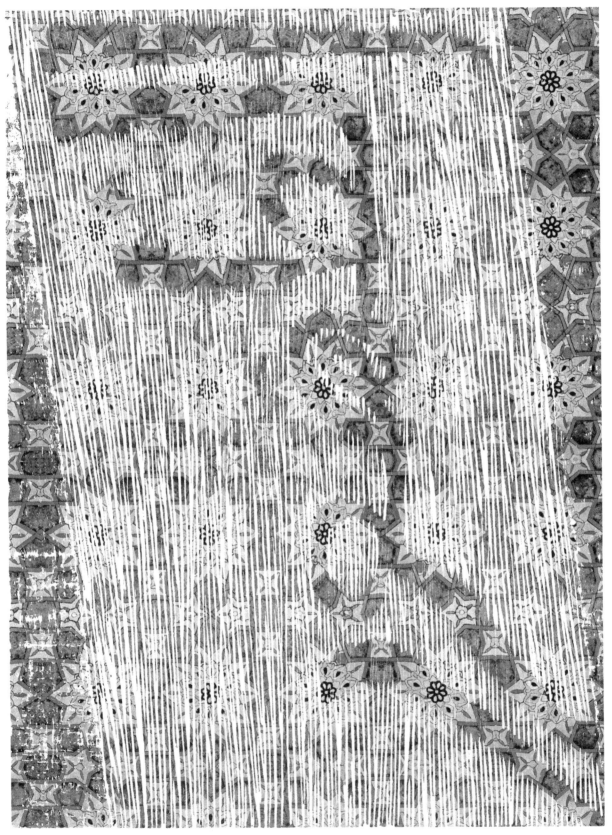

"Our abode in this world is transitory, our life therein but a loan, our breaths numbered and our indolence manifest."
Abu Bakr - Siddiqi

"Do not get elated at any victory, for all such victory is subject to the will of Allah."
Abu Bakr - Siddiqi

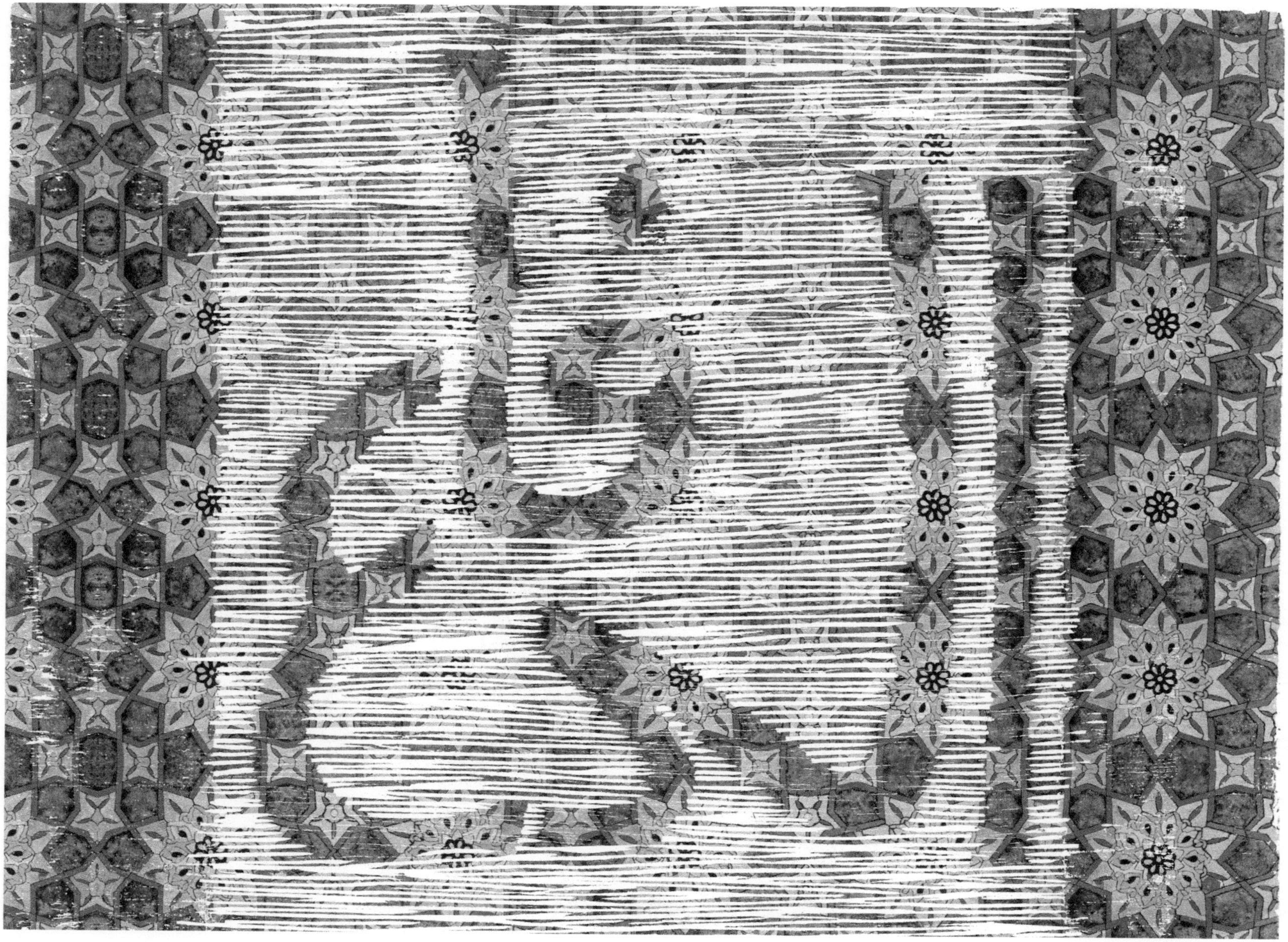

Al-Difa'a | Defence

Al-Kitman | Sacred Deception

"A wise man first thinks and then speaks
and a fool speaks first and then thinks."
Ali - Taliba

Imam

An islamic leader capable of doing both good & *bad*. Who studies the Quran & Sunnah as a religious *undergrad*. But everyone seems to have missed the Berber's female *comrade*.

Take the four imams and their visions as imadjïnn-ary *fuel*. For they are what mainly inspired Ibn-Rustam's Imamate of the first Persian Muslim's *rule*.

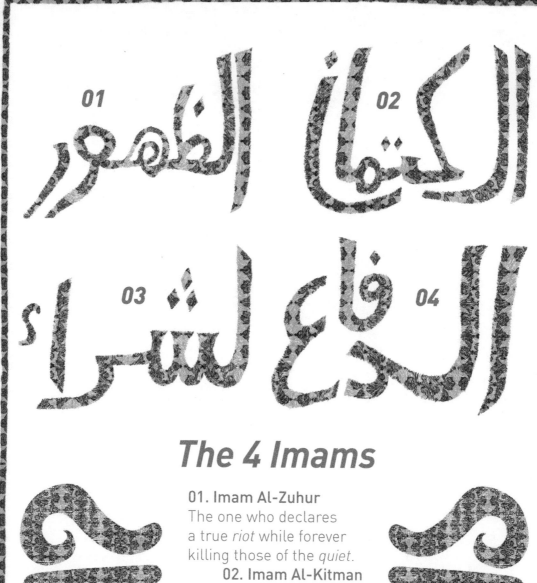

01 02 03 04

The 4 Imams

01. Imam Al-Zuhur
The one who declares
a true *riot* while forever
killing those of the *quiet*.
02. Imam Al-Kitman
The one that *deceives*
what everyone *believes*.
03. Imam Al-Shar'aa
She who incites the Ber-
ber's *fight* for equal *right*.
04. Imam Al-Dif'aa
The one that rises during
times of *revolt* to bring
forth Najda's critical *jolt*.

Rustam Ibn-Rouzbeh I Imam Al-Farsi

Ibn-Ibadh I follow your **Madhab, School Of Thought** with all my *heart* for it gave me four powers of the ancient *art*:

Declaration: The one who rises *first* shall hold the power of **Al-Zuhur** to quench a rebellious *thirst*. Their true ideas never shared with a fellow *rioteer*, so always be wary of the *pioneer* as they can often become a newly inspired *exiteer*.

Activism: When one incites a *fight* for equal *right* as a public *plight* there exists no better use of Allah's *might*. For the use of **Al-Sha'raa** in name of **Ahad, One *God*** is how you unmask a *fraud* the people have chosen to *applaud*.

Defence: When a home is under *attack*, then the power of **Al-Difa'a** will surely make someone's pacifism *crack*. For a millitary rule will always be the dream for every violent *tool*. But it is only a guarding force in Ibn-Ibadh's *school*.

Sacred Deception: Generally known as **Al-Kitman**, or *Taqiyah* if you are indeed *Shi'ah*. Where one is allowed to *conceil* their belief to make their life unable to *steal*. Over time it shall also be used as a trick to destroy and *heal*.

Imam Al-Farsi I Rustam Ibn-Rouzbeh

181

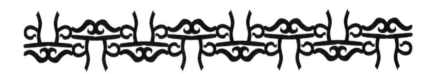

182

Salma Ibn Saad I Imam Al-Ifriqiya

The Byzantine Romans used to govern Ifriqiya as part of their African *empire*. But a series of decisive raids by the Umayad dynasty made this province a part of their ruling *wire*. Constantinois (East Algeria), Tripolitania (West Libya) and all of Tunisia were the territories of Ifriqiya's *fire*.

Twenty years before Maysara Al-Matghi declared the very first Berber Muslim Revolt in the 122nd Hijri *year*. I, Salma along with Rustam and a bunch of other Abadiyah **Imams, Islamic Guides** had finally arrived in Kairouan, Tunisia established by Uqba who was now no longer *here*. After Kusaila The Berber Leopard was able to form an alliance with Byzantine Romans to launch an ambush that made the lives of both Uqba and his 3.000 men *disappear*. An ambush known as the battle of Vescera which was fought during Yazid's *reign*. This defeat led to a free Tunisia for ten years until the Byzantine-Berber alliance was *slain*.

We used the four ancient powers of our Abadiyah *school*, to fire up the Berbers in their opposition towards Umayad *rule*. For we no longer think like the **Khawarij, Exiteers** who proved themselves to be no more than a violent *tool*.

Imam Al-Ifriqiya I Salma Ibn-Saad

Jabir Ibn-Zayd I Al-Mukhles 2.0

A student of both Aisha and Ibn-Abbas who managed to build his very own *creed*. By often disagreeing with his teachers and looking for answers by himself *indeed*. The one who truly paved the way for **Ijtihad, Individual Reasoning** to further spread the theological *seed*. He was born in the very first **Tabi'i, Follower** *year*. The newly inspired generation born right after the death of the messenger who the **Ümmah, Community** held so *dear*.

Ibn-Zayd used the power of **Al-Zuhur, Declaration** to openly state that he disagreed with Ibn-Ibadh leader of the Abadiyah *school*. If only he could have realised in time that Abd Al-Malik was simply using him as another blind *tool*. By getting one of his generals to befriend Ibn-Zayd while at he same time sending him a *spy*. As soon as he found out Ibn-Zayd called for the execution of this double agent no *lie*. This eventually *led* to Abd Al-Malik's unforeseen quest to completely sever Abadiyah's ideological *head*.

Over the entire city of Basrah, Iraq Abadiyah men were hunted *down*. Some killed, others captured and the rest escaped to Oman seeking refuge from the Umayad *crown*.

Al-Mukhles 2.0 I Jabir Ibn-Zayd

Maysara Al-Matghi I Imam Al-Zuhur

The Berbers had to accept a religion that benefited them in a theoretical *way*. But the Umayad dynasty's cultural practices solidified their status as second-class citizens who received extra taxes to *pay*. They were to be held down by Arab superiority until the very coming of judgement *day*. Until the **Imams, Islamic Guides** of the Abadiyah *school*, preached revolt to fire up berber resentment for a multicultural *rule*. But little did they know that the first rebel who would *rise* carried a hatred resembling Nafi's blue *eyes*. Maysara adopted the islamic faith and did everything he *could*, to completely do away with the idolatrous polytheism that was highly prevalent in his Berber *hood*.

But it still wasn't enough to achieve a position of governing in Ifriqiya's *land*. So he took a page from the defeated Azariqa mindset and set up a barbarically rebellious *command*. Never again would they accept a shrewd Arab telling them what to *do*, as the Berber leader Maysara truly became obsessed with the vengeful mindset of the *blue*.

From Tangiers, Morocco Al-Matghi declared a rebellion so *gritty* in an attempt to conquer Kairouan the Ifriqiyan *city*.

Imam Al-Zuhur I Maysara Al-Matghi

184

Abd Allah Ibn-Ibadh I Al-Tamimi 2.0

Abd Al-Malik came between the dynamic duo that tried to build a school unlike any *other*. But Ibn-Ibadh knew that Ibn-Zayd would one day go against him as that is usually what happens when you work so closely with a fellow Muslim *brother*. Especially when you take into account Ibn-Ibadh's inspiration to build the pillars of the Abadiyah *school*. Was only acquired after he had studied Ibn-Zayd's wonderfully written Diwan *tool*. But now that book was sadly no *more*, as Abd Al-Malik ordered every single copy to be destroyed in an attempt to fully settle the *score*.

Al-Diwan was the first book of **Fiqh, Religious *Law*** that was written by a man who could enlighten any scholarly *flaw*. After it was gone from this *land*, Ibn-Zayd chose to no longer write anything with his *hand*. But rather he educated his students of islamic history by using **Al-Hadith, Assembled Reports** of the messenger's time of *command*. Reports that required critical thinking to *go* with the *flow*.

As he taught his students those lessons Ibn-Ibadh chose to focus on his master plan that the Umayad dynasty was yet to *know*. In which Arabs will be viewed as the real *foe*.

Al-Tamimi 2.0 I Abd Allah Ibn-Ibadh

185

Abd Ar Rahman Ibn-Rustam I Imam Al-Kitman

When Khattabo invaded the Sassanian Persian *empire*, anger & resentment were what caused Piruz's hatred to *transpire*. Many high-quality servants were enslaved without *wait*, and if their Arab master was sly enough he could enter them through Medina's *gate*. But as much as I respect Khattabo's *rule* there were some mistakes he made after certain followers of his managed to play him as a *fool*. Giving way for injustice to spread as a vile *tool*.

While Khattabo desperately searched for Fatima's grave during each medinan *night*. He failed to realise that it was the Persian slaves who cursed his Arab throne of *might*. As they were being taxed so much it often left them unable to *eat*. And the rough manual labour they were forced to do kept making blisters grow on both their hands and *feet*.

If only Luqman The Wise could've chosen to speak to him about this *crime*, knowing Khattabo he would have surely done something to punish such impermissible *grime*. But Luqman chose to stay silent and it filled him up with *hate*. Seeking a way to brutalise Khattabo without *wait*, it seems as though history is repeating itself with the Berber *fate*.

Imam Al-Kitman I Abd Ar Rahman Ibn-Rustam

Dihya Al-Kahina I Umm-Amazigh

When the disciple's son launched a rebelllion of magnitude against the truly mad Umayad *king*. I felt inspired to incite the same kind of revolt by making the Berber pride rise up and *sing*. I negotiated a deal between my ally and the Byzantines to fight against the invading *forces*. The battle of Vescera in which we nearly doubled Uqba's army both in fighters and horses. And it actually managed to *work* until the alliance was disturbed by a Byzantine *jerk*.

Sadly my ally Kusaila The Berber Leopard's blood was *spilled* three years after Uqba and his 3.000 troops were *killed*. During my ally's last day of *life* the Umayad king Abd Al-Malik had just finished his first ruling year in *strife*. In his seventh year of rule one of his generals actually managed to kill the disciple's *son*. He was beheaded and chained to a cross for 11 months until his very old mother Asma The Brave was allowed to bury her martyred *one*.

After that moment of *time*, the leader within me awakened to save my Berber people from the Umayad dynasty's endless series of *crime*. For I shall be known as a Berber queen who stood against the Umayads and their *grime*.

Umm-Amazigh I Dihya Al-Kahina

187

Sajah Bint Al-Kahina I Imam Al-Sha'raa

O mother you were the very first queen who was able to establish an independent Berber *state*. While the Umayad general Musa Bin Nusayr used to call you **Al-Kahina, The Soothsayer** with an oracling ability to tell *fate*. Hoping it would make sure the Berber Muslims who fought beside you would treat you with the utmost *hate*. But that strategy horribly failed and thus it was abandoned without *wait*.

You established your state three years after the death of the disciple's *son* who was killed as an unlucky *one*. From that very moment the Umayad *forces* stormed your territory with more than a thousand Arabian *horses*. But for five years you managed to rule from the Aures Mountains to the Oasis of Gadames in a manner so *free*. Back then I was still an idolatrous deity that sat on your lap as if I were an 'idol' for all of the Berbers to *see*. If only you could have lived long enough to witness the manifestation that is *me*.

But sadly that was impossible after Musa The Umayad General came back with more men in accordance with Abd Al-Malik's *decree*. You fought until you *died* in the Roman amphitheater of Al-Djem as my heart surely *cried*.

Imam Al-Sha'raa I Sajah Bint Al-Kahina

188

Najda Ibn-Amir I Abu-Najadat

When the **Muhakkima, Unjudged** became **Khawarij, Exiteers** there existed four main *streams* built by a singular leader's undying *dreams*. **Sufriya, Yellowfaced** who came to existence by following Ibn-Zayd's *path*. Azariqa whose founder Nafi created a rigidly terrifying mindset as a suggestion of Allah's *wrath*. Abadiyah of Ibn-Ibadh who eventually teamed up with Ibn-Zayd to create a multifunctional *school*. And lastly a faction built by me Najda who sought to completely do away with a **Caliph, Successor** *rule*.

Apparently when I was a young boy several apostates rose up to *rebel*, this happened during Siddiqi's reign when I was still a little baby protected from the flames of *hell*. One of the apostates Musaylimah had built a following in Al-Yamamah which was currently under Umayad *jurisdiction*. But that didn't stop me from causing the necessary *friction*. I conquered Al-Yamamah and gave the Umayad governors a peaceful *eviction*. For I also criticised Nafi's terrifying killing *addiction*. For the first time a house was built without a religious *helm*, for I was the founder of Najadat who preferred to *overwhelm*. If only I could have been murdered by someone from outside of my small *realm*."

Abu-Najadat I Najda Ibn-Amir

190

Abdu-Amazigh I Imam Al-Difa'a

I was the house servant of a Berber Chieftain family from the highest *blood*, but then the Umayad forces continually stormed our lands giving way for a barbaric river of red to *flood*. From Kairouan, Tunisia to Tangiers, Morocco that was the Ifriqiya of Uqba's *dreams*. But even after half a century the Umayads were unable to conquer Morocco especially now that Maysara rose up to burst through the rebellious *seams*. He preached with the utmost *hate* as to him it was the only emotion that was strong enough to make sure equality forever becomes our permanent *fate*.

But I myself saw through Maysara's blue inspired *lies*, especially when I read the public critique of Najda Ibn-Amir against Nafi Ibn Al-Azraq's mindset which he had branded as extremely sinful Iblisian Tactics in *disguise*. He clearly believed that it was completely unnecessary to have one **Caliph, Successor** to lead the islamic *school*. Those that believed it was necessary were branded by Najda as a *fool*.

Maysara may have started the rebellion in Tangiers, Morocco but he was killed rather *fast*. By the rebels that I turned against him in a sermon where I recalled the *past*.

Imam Al-Difa'a I Abdu-Amazigh

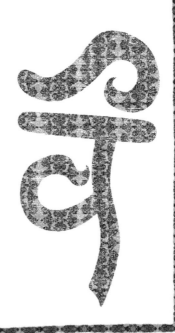

The Arab

The emigrators of North Africa's mysterious *land*. Undoing queen Dihya Al-Kahina's reign to place the Berbers under Umayad *command*. Which lead to another class society completely going against the messenger's *demand*.

A society that was destroyed by the hatching of The Abadiyah *Eggs*. Giving the resistance stable *legs*.

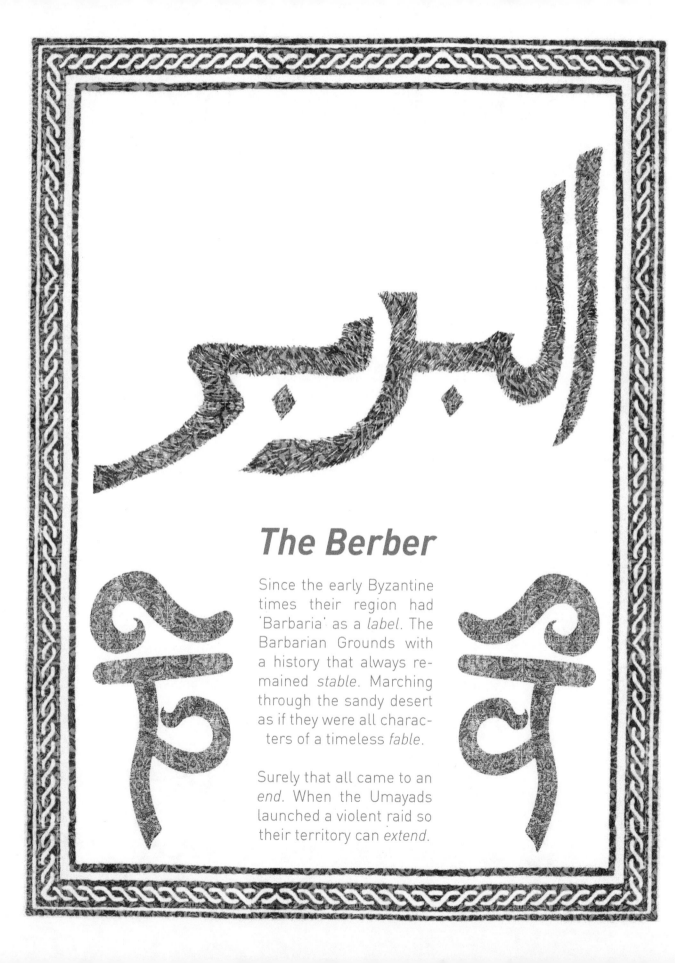

The Berber

Since the early Byzantine times their region had 'Barbaria' as a *label*. The Barbarian Grounds with a history that always remained *stable*. Marching through the sandy desert as if they were all characters of a timeless *fable*.

Surely that all came to an *end*. When the Umayads launched a violent raid so their territory can *extend*.

191

Sajah Bint Al-Kahina I Imam Al-Sha'raa

O mother when you lost the battle you also lost your *head*. Never returned back to your people but rather given to Abd Al-Malik as a trophy *instead*. I was dying away on the ground until a Berber Muslim picked me up and filled my wooden idol with *glee*. It was as if I felt the power of the three meccan chief goddesses who converted to the islamic *plea*. Al-Lat, Al-'Uzza and Manat all three joining themselves in the wooden doll that is *me*. I was another deity of the wider DJ'inn *population*. That chose to shift shape towards the supernatural piety of the Musdjïnn's *nation*. So from the very moment this Berber Muslim held me in his *hand*, I poetically inspired his brain's *command*.

"O Berbers let us build a shrine for our Berber queen who fought until her last *breath*. For her bravery will make sure our women will never allow her legacy to suffer a neglectful *death*. I hear there exists a faction of **Khawarij, Exiteers** where excessive devotion is *key*. So let us build a yellow temple on top of Dihya's grave where we can place Sajah for everyone to *see*. But bear in *mind* that Sajah the Berber doll shall only become reality when she is accepted by a pious individual from a different exiteering *kind*."

Imam Al-Sha'raa I Sajah Bint Al-Kahina

The Abbasid Revolution
746 - 750 J

Sajah Bint Al-Kahina I Imam Al-Sha'raa

Ibn-Rustam swore a pledge to *me* in front of all my Berber followers to *see*. At first they were suspicious of him because of his Persian *skin*. But then his interpretation of the **Mahdi, Messiah** theory made their loyalties his to *win*.

Shi'ah - Succession By Blood

The messiah must come from the messenger's *house*, if not then a revolt will happen in which none will stay silent as a *mouse*. **Ahl-Al-Bayt, The People Of The house** *indeed*, who choose to further build on Hashim's generous *seed*.

Sunnah - Succession By Water

The entire Quraish tribe was eligible for the truest messiah to *rise*. As the messenger was sent to all of them as a mercy in *disguise*. The fact that it had to be of Hashim's house were merely fairytales formed by suspicious *lies*.

Abadiyah - Succession By Air

The many different narrations of the messenger's farewell message clearly *say*. That Arab superiority is unnecessary *anyway*. Our religion is spreading all accross the *earth*, so therefore it should never matter who you were at *birth*.

Imam Al-Sha'raa I Sajah Bint Al-Kahina

192

The Imadjïnnary Narrator
129 - 132 H

Walid Ibn-Yazid (II) I Walid II

The establishment of Siddiqi and Khattabo's *school* led to an islamic empire of electionary *rule*. But then Muawiyah made sure the Rashidun reign was no *more*. After he lied to make Hasan Ibn Asadullah draw up a peace treaty to settle the *score*. Muawiyah became the first to build a monarchy that only the shrewdest Arabs chose to *adore*.

193

1st: Muawiyah (I) Ibn Abi-Sufyan	*661 - 680 J*
2nd: Yazid Ibn-Muawiyah	*680 - 683 J*
3rd: Muawiyah (II) Ibn-Yazid	*683 - 684 J*
4th: Marwan Ibn Al-Hakam	*684 - 685 J*
5th: Abd Al-Malik Ibn Marwan	*685 - 705 J*
6th: Al-Walid (I) Ibn Abd Al-Malik	*705 - 715 J*
7th: Sulayman Ibn Abd Al-Malik	*715 - 717 J*
8th: Umar Ibn Abd Al-Aziz	*717 - 720 J*
9th: Yazid (II) Bin Abd Al-Malik	*720 - 724 J*
10th: Hisham Ibn Abd Al-Malik	*724 - 743 J*
11th: Al-Walid (II) Ibn-Yazid (II)	*743 - 744 J*
12th: Yazid (III) Ibn Al-Walid (II)	*744 - 744 J*
13th: Ibrahim Ibn Al-Walid (II)	*744 - 744 J*
14th: Marwan (II) Ibn-Muhammad	*744 - 750 J*

Walid II I Walid Ibn-Yazid

194

Marwan Ibn-Muhammad I Al-Marwani II

Affanu's reign in the **Rashidun, Rightly Guided** *empire* was a cocoon that made sure the Umayad dynasty was able to *transpire*. As Muawiyah and Marwan were both cousins of Affanu who promoted the silently obedient *creed*. Both of them were hungry to establish a rule based on their merciless *greed*. But Al-Sufyani eventually came *first* making Al-Marwani highly impatient to quench his ruling *thirst*.

About sixty years ago Al-Marwani had usurped his cousin Al-Sufyani's *rule*, by patiently awaiting the expected demise of Yazid the craziest *tool*. And when Yazid's son Muawiyah II took charge Al-Marwani easily brainwashed this young *fool*. As to the public Marwan was always known as the son of a man **Al-Hakam, The Judge** was his *name*. Seeking to completely undo Allah's presence by building his own *claim*. It was only natural that the second coming would seek to replay this form of slippery *fame*.

The third Fitna was launched by overthrowing Walid II who was the 11th **Caliph, Successor** of the Umayad *time*. And when Marwan II had risen to power as the 14th he tried anything to take back rebel territory no matter the *crime*.

Marwan II I Marwan Ibn-Muhammad

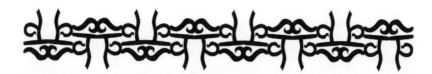

195

Abu-Muslim Al-Khorasani I Vehzadan Hormoz

When Ibn-Rustam told me how he and his fellow Abadiyah **Imams, Islamic Guides** preached puritanical *fire*. I myself felt the need to launch a rebellion in an attempt to *inspire*. For expanding a Muslim rule by the use of Persian administration is something to which I shall always *aspire*. For I truly am the proudest resident of Khorasan, Persia who believed that it was very much needed to retell certain ancient values of our previously Zoroastrian *empire*.

Muawiyah was a scribe of Muhammad who swore that the theory of a **Mahdi, Messiah** defeating **Dajjal, Anti-Messiah** was *real*. Even though there's not a single mention of it in the Quran's eternal *deal*. Was it not all part of a *lie* that managed to make the dynasty of Umayads rule our *sky*?

In that case the only way to undo that crooked *fable* is by finding the best candidate who was more than *able*. To take on the unique Mahdi's *goal* and kill off the fake Dajjal's harmful slaughterings of Muhammad's character and *soul*. When **As-Saffah, The Bloodshedder** demanded a **Bayah** from *me*, I gave my **Pledge** for everyone to *see*. Then I adopted the black *flag* of this Mahdi-Dajjal *drag*.

Vehzadan Hormoz I Abu-Muslim Al-Khorasani

Abd Allah Ibn Ali I Abu-Abbasid

One year after my nephew **As-Saffah, The Bloodshedder** marched to Kufa, Iraq and declared his **Caliphate, Succession** in front of every resident's *face*. The decisive battle near the great river of Zab, Iraq took *place*. The 35.000 Abbasid soldiers commanded by *me*, fought a much greater army of 135.000 Umayad soldiers but in the end Allah decided that our side would walk away with the *victory*.

The Umayad dynasty's morale had suffered from far more than one crack during this third rebellious *time*. And when we won the battle Marwan II fled to Damascus hoping he could be free of an execution filled with *grime*. But I would never let someone go unpunished after so much *crime*. Along with my soldiers I followed him and took the Syrian capital by *force*, but Marwan II already fled to Palestine after mounting his *horse*. I sent my brother Salih to finish him in one swift *move*. He was found in a small Egyptian town and his head was severed for my eyes to *prove*.

Now the people will hail **As-Saffah, The Bloodshedder** without *wait*. For he is the first **Caliph, Successor** of the Abbasids that killed off the Umayads of greed & *hate*.

Abu-Abbasid I Abd Allah Ibn Ali

196

Abu-Jafar Abd Allah Ibn Muhammad I Al-Mansuri

As-Saffah, The Bloodshedder's younger *brother* who also claimed descendancy from Ibn-Abbas the professor unlike any *other*. I remember very well that the Berber Muslim Revolt ended as a *fail*. But Hisham, the tenth **Caliph, Successor** of the Umayad dynasty died just a few months later after the stressful years of revolt made his ruined life *wail*.

Then Hisham's nephew Al-Walid II was appointed successor and he lasted about a *year*. Until Yazid III overthrew him in an honest attempt to make the Umayad injustice *disappear*. But Allah gave this son of a Persian princess and Umayad man only six months *time*. Until his body would flounder from a brain tumor of painful *grime*.

Then Ibrahim ruled for a short time as the 13th until Marwan II rose up without *wait*. But at that same time the Persian Ibn-Rustam mysteriously stormed through Mecca's *gate*. At last there is confirmation of the secret Abadiyah *society*, who informed its leaders whether or not the meccans held on to their *piety*. Marwan II tried to roughly subdue them at *first* but ruling tensions in Damascus, Syria forced him to accept Abadiyah's truly rebellious *thirst*.

Al-Mansuri I Abu-Jafar Abd Allah Ibn Muhammad

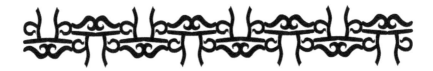

Abu Al-Abbas As-Saffah I Al-Abbasidi

Ibn-Rustam truly convinced me that my potential claim of the **Caliphate, Succession** was of the highest *degree*. So I marched toward Kufa, Iraq and presented its highly rebellious residents with my ruling *decree*. Both Sunnis and Shi'ahs came to the conclusion that I was the *best*. For my descendancy of the great professor Ibn-Abbas outweighed that of all the *rest*. In both interpretations I am considered as righteous and *just*. Now all that is left to do is defeat the Umayads who have fallen to the sinful ways of *lust*.

When my uncle commanded our Abbasid forces in the decisive battle of Zab and actually *won*. My heart nearly jumped out of my chest as I imadjïnned the vast potentials of my ruling *fun*. By the time I arrived in Damascus, Syria it had already been taken over by *him*. That's when I held a vast ceremony where the people would now praise the Abbasidian *hymn*. Now racial minorities would be given the chance to lead their own *school*. But an Arab commander will always and forever remain at the true head of a *rule*.

Those who stood with the pathetic Umayad dynasty should always have *fear*, for the Abbasid dynasty is finally *here*.

Al-Abbasidi I Abu Al-Abbas As-Saffah

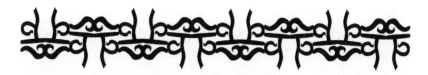

198

The Third Wave Of Fitna
744 - 747 J

Abd Ar Rahman Ibn-Rustam I Imam Al-Kitman

After Maysara rebelled in a manner that went against my *creed*, I used the Abadiyah powers to grow my own *seed*.

Al-Zuhur - Declaration
I was the one who met with **As-Saffah, The Bloodshedder** and informed him that his claim would be the *best*. As his Ibn-Abbas bloodline would outweigh that of all the *rest*.

Al-Sha'raa - Activism
When the Abbasid commander Al-Khorasani felt highly inspired by the Berber Revolt so *tough*. I fired up his fantasies giving his rebellion a necessary mindset so *rough*.

Al-Difa'a - Defence
The late Ibn-Ibadh didn't just go to Mecca to help the disciple's son keep it *intact*. But rather to further spread the non-conflicting teachings of the strong Abadiyah *pact*.

Al-Kitman - Sacred Deception
I fooled the Sufriya Berbers by pledging that I truly believe in their Sajah *doll*. But they have no idea that I am merely making sure that the Abadiyah teachings will never *fall*.

Imam Al-Kitman I Abd Ar Rahman Ibn-Rustam

The Imadjinnary Narrator
126 - 129 H

The Abbasid Revolution
746 - 750 J

Abd Ar Rahman Ibn-Rustam I Imam Al-Kitman

I had inspired the recent revolts by bringing a Persian in-spiration to it *all*. How painful it must be for the Umayads to know that their legacy has come to a destructive *fall*. **As-Saffah, The Bloodshedder** had slaughtered all of their perverted *blood*, making sure that a barbaric river of red was able to *flood*. This all to completely do away with the Umayad *creed* of Arab superiority and merciless *greed*.

Now that the Abbasid dynasty has been estalished without *wait*, I can finally focus on building an empire where my Persian skin is what leads the people's *fate*. A dynasty of Rustamids where diversity is far more than a political *tool*. As I am the second coming of Luqman The Wise who al-ways belonged to his very own house in a manner so *cool*.

I, Abd Ar Rahman Ibn-Rustam shall be known as the first Persian to build an Ifriqiyan Abadiyah *school*. Where it is not necessary to make an Arab the man to *rule*, as our re-cent history has proven that anyone can be both a genius and a *fool*. Ibn-Ibadh's poetic *sway* is what truly leads my *way*. For all of the people are made equal in Allah's meta-phorical *eyes* that forever witness everything in the *skies*.

Imam Al-Kitman I Abd Ar Rahman Ibn-Rustam

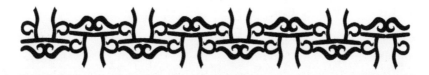

200

The Imadjinnary Narrator
129 - 132 H

"In the matter of justice, all should
be equal in your eyes."
Abu Bakr - Siddiqi

"Recitation of the Quran without con-
templation and thought is futile."
Ali - Taliba

"When knowledge is limited it leads to folly, but when it exceeds a certain limit there is great risk of exploitation."
Abu Bakr - Siddiqi

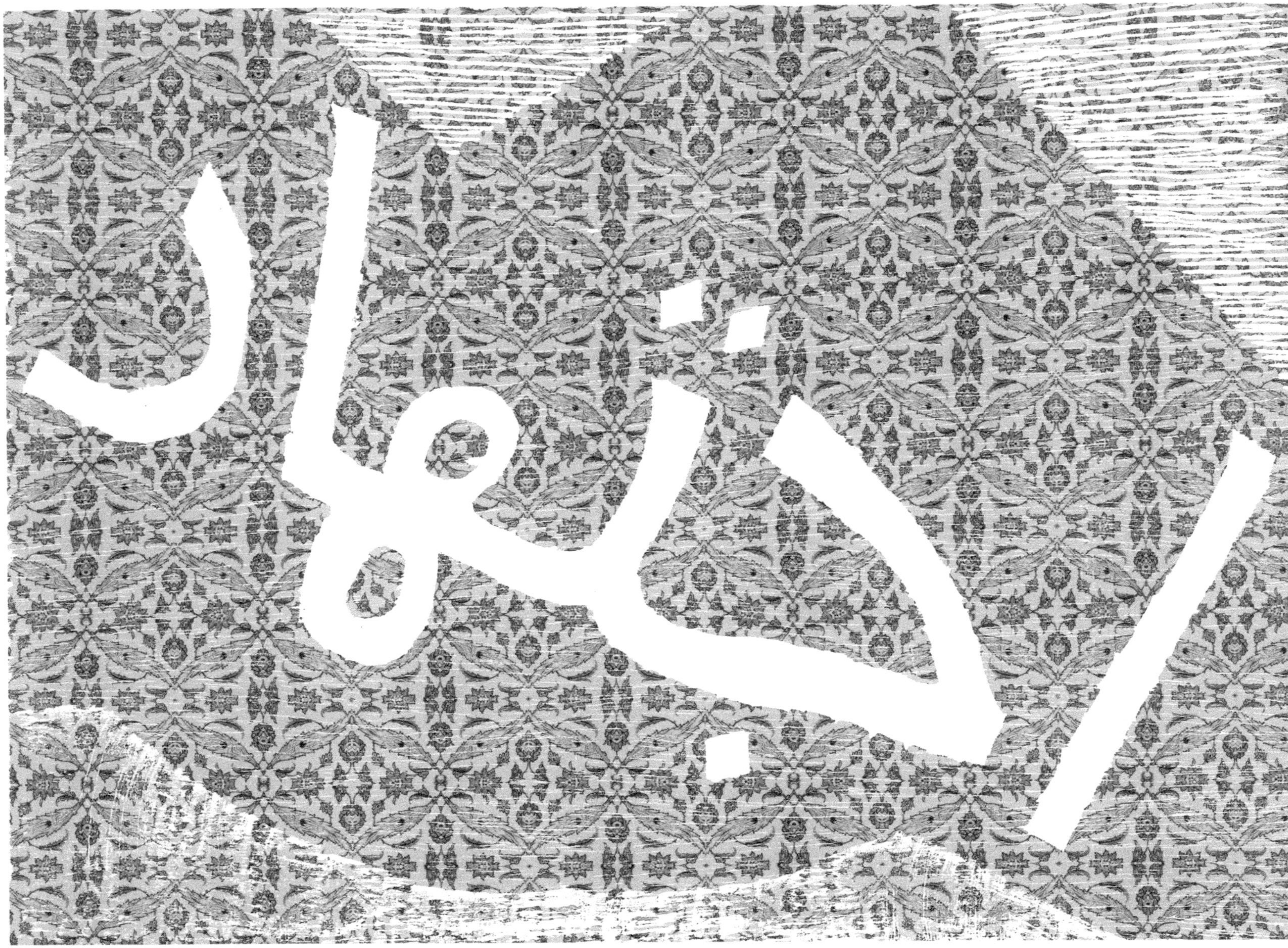

Ijtihad | Individual Reasoning

"Prefer for the people what you prefer for yourself. What you do not wish for yourself, do not impose on others."
Umar - Khattabo

"Take note of the fact that I am a follower of religious tradition and not at all an innovator."

Uthman - Affanu

Ijma | Unanimous Reasoning

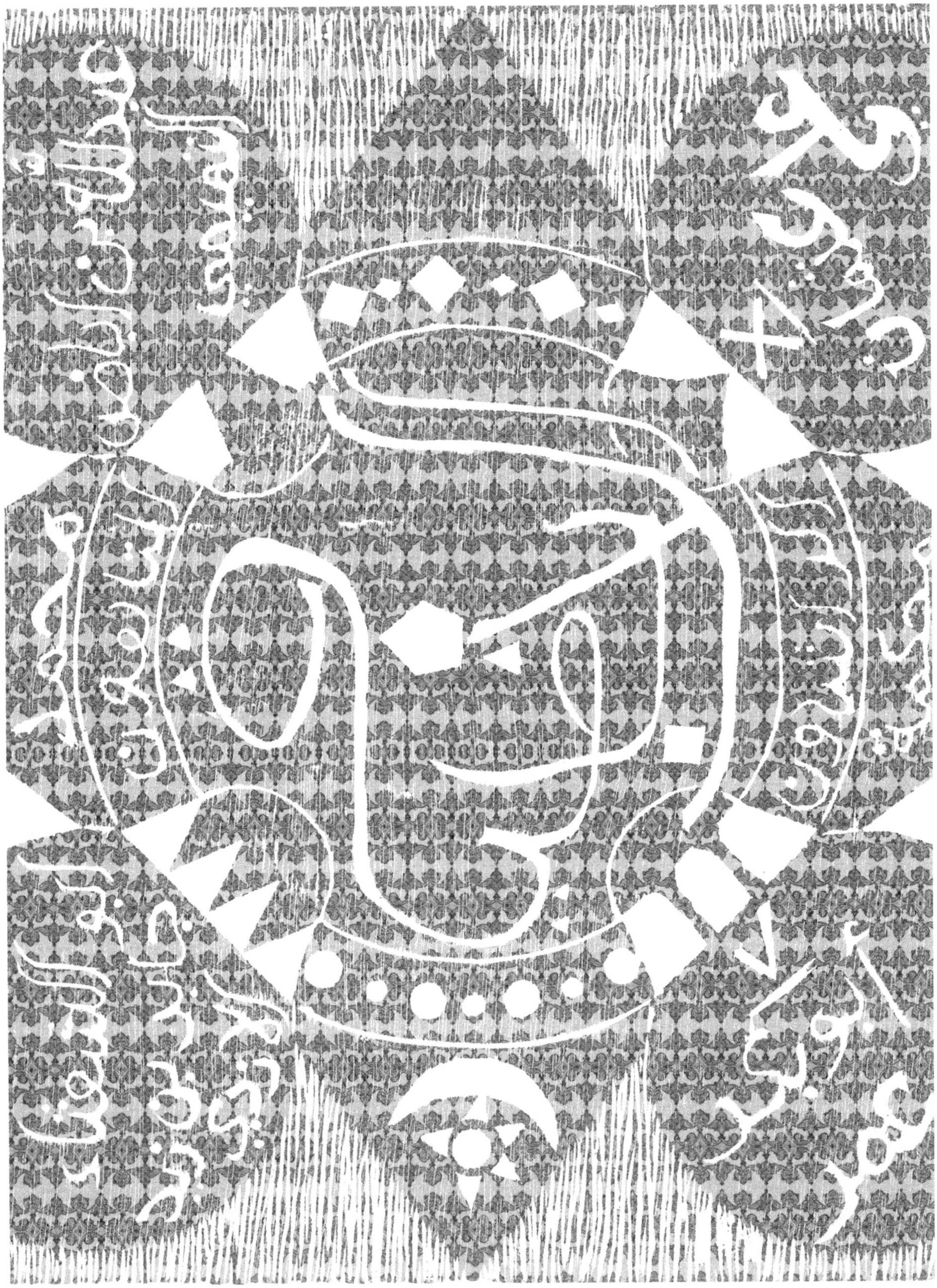

Quran Verse 02: The Cow

256. Let there be no compulsion in religion: For truth will always stand out clear from *error*. Whoever rejects evil and believes in Allah has the most trustworthy hand-hold that never breaks by the pressures of *terror*. For Allah hears and sees *all* so make sure that your loyalties never experience a *downfall*."

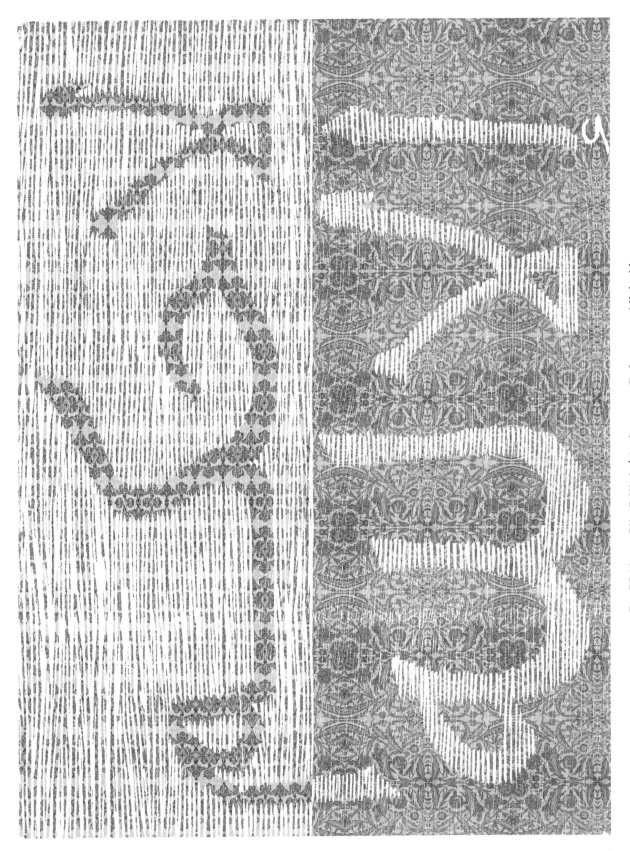

La Hukma Illa Lillah | *Judgement Belongs to Allah Alone*

Lightning Source UK Ltd.
Milton Keynes UK
UKHW051153020619

343606UK00005B/137/P